THE
COLLECTED POEMS
OF
WILSON CLOUGH

McNaughton & Gunn, Inc
Saline, Michigan 48176-0010

ISBN: 0-941570-11-8
Library of Congress 90-071007

PREFACE

I HAVE NEVER LABELED MYSELF a Poet, in the sense of a lifetime of dedication to the art. Numerous duties and modesty prevented. Nevertheless, as a teacher of language and literature, I assumed that, like the teacher of music, one should practice the instrument. For there is more to literature than merely the reading. The poet must think of language, words, connotations, pace, harmony in sound, rejection of the too obvious, and the finality of meaning. A poem is not a whole philosophy — nothing so formidable — but an exploration of an idea, a mood, a fragment of the richness of life. It must have some freshness of conception, a concreteness beneath metaphor.

Two small books of poems have been previously issued. The first was published in 1954, entitled *Brief Oasis*, printed by the Allan Swallow Press of Denver. Swallow had been a former student of mine. The next edition, of some 70 poems, appeared in 1972, when I was 78. It was privately issued from the University of Wyoming Publications, and entitled *Past's Persisting*, and locally distributed. I had thought that final, but a few since appear to merit salvaging.

From habit in teaching, I have not hesitated to add in the Appendix certain comments. An asterisk on any title indicates such. The latest additions called for a minimum of revision of position. Dates following a poem are, first the date of final composition; and second, date of publication, outside of book publications above.

Acknowledgments to magazines which have published one or another of the poems are due to: *American Scholar, Arizona Quarterly, Colorado Quarterly, Frontier and Midland, Lyric West, Massachusetts Review, News Letter* (College English Ass'n), *New Mexico Quarterly, Oregonian, Pacific Spectator, Prairie Schooner, Prism International, Rocky Mt. Review* (later *Western Humanities Review*), *Saturday Review Of Literature.* Add: Haiku in a Japanese-English magazine in Japan; and three poems translated into French and in *Europe* (Paris).

Many generous friends merit my thanks. But here I must be content to record a very special indebtedness to two women. They are Mrs. David (Jane) Love and her daughter Frances Froidevaux. Between them, they most thoroughly examined the text for literary or grammatical slips in French or English. I found them most accurate and knowledgable, and I sincerely welcome this opportunity to say, "I thank you.."

IN MEMORIAM
LAURA BOWMAN CLOUGH
(1895-1961)

INTRODUCTION

MEMORIES OF WILSON CLOUGH date from the autumn of 1956. The School of American Studies was holding one of its annual picnics at Hidden Valley. I observed a wiry, intense, bespectacled academician leaning against a picnic table, engaged in the perpetual ping pong debate that academics so relish — publish or perish. At last came the soft, staccato sentence, "Well, all I can say is that the faculty should do something or perish!" The finality of the statement turned the subject to fishing the Snowy Range, the irony being lost on most.

Wilson Clough first came on the Laramie scene in 1924. Clough not only felt comfortable in this 7,000-foot plus atmosphere, but joined with gusto the frequent intellectual jousts on such subjects as Newton and gravity, Kant and rationalism, economic history of 18th century France, John Locke, etc.

With far-ranging, free-wheeling intellect, Clough added both spirit and lustre to the intellectual life of the University and its town. Clough juggled the demands of twelve-hour teaching load, production of a stream of publications, and chairmanship of the English Department. The harvest arrived in a parade of students (some appreciative of the exposure to Clough's mental gymnastics, some bewildered and frightened). All the while, Clough scribbled the mental delights which danced in his head, resulting in two of the finest and most quoted works in American Intellectual history — *Our Long Heritage,* and *The Necessary Earth.* These two volumes reflected Clough's lifetime concern with intellectual origins or philosophical roots.

It is a pleasure to present *The Collected Poems of Wilson Clough* with our delight, appreciation, and deep respect for the author.

Gene M. Gressley
June 28, 1990

Wilson Clough

TABLE OF CONTENTS

PART I. Earlier Poems (1926-1953)

PART II. War's Alarms (1918-1945)

PART III. Of Wyoming (1934-1948)

PART IV. Of Foreign Tongues (1919-1969)

PART V. Times of Loss (1944-1969)

PART VI. Poems Since Fifty (1944-1973)

PART VII. Late Harvest (Since 1973)

ADDENDA

APPENDIX

BIOGRAPHICAL NOTE

PART I
EARLIER POEMS
(1925-1953)

NEW ENGLAND BIRCH

Now ALL THE waking, stone-walled lands
Gaze silent where the forest stands;
For here, against the evergreen
That lift their dusky, circling screen,
A native wood-nymph, white and slim,
With grace upon each slender limb,
Fashions a breathless, tip-toe pose,
And beauty's fragile image glows.

But Nature here has reprimands:
For even as the marvel grows,
New England skies, reproachful, grim,
Lower a virtuous veil of snows.

(1926, 1936)

ALL WORDS

ALL WORDS that mouths may form have truth. The word
That gropes and falters short of accents sure
Confesses past dispute that life has stirred
Beneath the uncouth sign, the hint obscure.
The child's clear note, the mob's low-throated roar,
The pedant's phrase, the phantoms books have bred—
Each still has this: Life spoke. The word's no more,
Not having life, than walls untenanted.

Nothing that men can say is wholly lie:
For let them shout their thoughts or shroud them deep,
Each lifted hand, each syllable, each sigh,
Has deepest springs; and patient mind may leap
From crafty tongue or laboring commonplace
To scan the cryptic scrolls of time and space.

(1933, 1941)

CARL SANDBURG PROGRAM *

THEN HE CAME,
With a quick, lithe tread
Of a man who could stir his stumps,
And a frugal, pithy frame
Trim for bouts with old flint-heart Time.
Under his lancer's pennon drooping iron grey,
Grey eyes held steady
As the sun's grave gaze through morning mists.
Swaying to some inner rhythm,
His comments came, in a casual, mellow key,
On will-o-the-wisps and hard tack,
On tough guys and rainbows,
On cabooses, and swamps that lie
Lonely and lovely under the stars.

He chanted low-down songs,
Beach-comber tunes and negro songs,
Touching soft chords on his handy guitar,
Mm-plinkety-plank-plank, mm-plunk-plunk;
Till you saw him squatting by a hobo fire
Serenading the moon,
Not giving a damn for proper folk.

Butter-and-egg men were trapped in a chuckle
In the Village of Liver-and-Onions.
Flapper folly knew a strange moment of wonder
At this mad, sad, fair world of ours.
In some dreamland a shadow dancer gestured free,
Strewing—was it biscuits or hyacinths?

John Doe, citizen, standard U.S.A.
(Cash register tinkle was music enough),
Cleared his throat and stirred at the lure and insistent beat
Of an outcast rhyme from the tattered fringes of money-folk.

The asterisk indicates a note in the Appendix.

4

But hard eyes stared at the platform singer
From here and there
Like hawks to pounce on a light-pink rat,
Any unguarded yawp at the status-quo;
Scowling, growling, "Say, who does he think he is?"
Say, Carl Sandburg,
Loafer, Swede, toiler, poet, melter of frozen words,
Who the hell do you think you are?

(February 1929, 1949)

ON THE DEATH
OF THE BRILLIANT MR. MOORE
(Who Succumbed while Pursuing the Ph.D.)

MOORE KNEW MORE than most, 'twas said;
Moore longed for more, now Moore is dead.
Had Moore known less, he might still be;
Now we know more, though less than he.

(1933. 1949)

NOT SO ARDENT

FAITHFUL to the myth, who'll try
    Lip and breast in feverish sort,
Thinking thus to justify
    Strumpet fiction's quaint report.

Not so ardent is the fact.
    Time's assessment has preferred
The reconnaissance exact,
    The immedicable word.

Beneath body, blood and brain
    Dwells the solitary bone,
Here the antique Stoic strain,
    Here the pilgrimage alone.

(1941, 1949)

EQUATION

Two APPREHENSIONS there are:
To reach and fall short of the star;
To grasp, and consent to the scar.
These the twin opposites are.

(1942, 1954)

NEW ENGLAND MAID

Her eyes are clear and candid, cool
As a mountain pool
Where slender grasses lift as if
No flood had ever stormed that cliff;
Where small translucencies do glide
Across that blue-inverted tide,
Or, at a shadow, dart within
On frosted fin.

(1943)

PHILOSOPHER ON OLYMPUS

(Note: Josephus relates that when the Roman soldiers burst into the Holy of Holies of the temple in Jerusalem, expecting to find treasure, they gazed only on the bare rock upon which the temple was built.)

Truncate, Olympus sulked in ominous cloud.
Believers moaned before the mercy seat,
And panic whispers ran the anxious crowd
To blame the circumstance on impious feet.
For, fool or wise man, who would risk the wrath
Of storm, right-mindedness or gods, to climb
Where piety had carved no previous path,
And vengeance stalked the old Promethean crime?
Thus sudden fists bit hard on sullen stone
When he came down; and all thought he'd confess;
But he passed on, as he had climbed, alone,
Whilst they disputed sin or holiness.
And none to ask the vision he might share:
The glory of a peak, sky-swept and bare.

(1936, 1938)

6

DARK ROBES

DARK ROBES, their temples dim and chill within,
Thunder the threadbare curse on candid doubt,
Invoke the formula for prideful sin
If mind's appraising glance fall less devout;
Still shaping virtue out of barrenness,
Abuse poor flesh as devil's advocate,
Congeal their Truth in one set mold and dress,
And guard with eyes regrettably like hate.
The faithful gestures grow mechanical,
The hallowed phrases foreign and antique;
For how shall one scant creed encompass all,
Frail symbols, long embalmed, be aught but weak,
When monstrous clouds, mushrooming stark dismay,
Roll up their heavy frown above our clay?

(1946)

INCIDENT ON THE AVENUE

"I, TOO, A MINIM in this milling host,
Confess I'm not the clearly purposed man
You'd think. That's what exacerbates her most—
My lingering flair for some considerate plan."
We stepped within a niche of plated glass.
"It seems I'm gallant. That she can't abide."
Brooding, he gazed upon a waxen lass
Who blessed the lingerie of Eastertide
And proffered gracile arms involved in furs.
"But whether world events absolve my state—
Or whether mine's the blame as much as hers—
Or why the world and weakness end in hate—"
The wind grew chill. Beneath the pithless girl
The black soot wound its flawless spiral swirl.

(1948)

TIGER ON THE ROAD

"Truly men hate the truth: They'd liefer
Meet a tiger on the road." Robinson Jeffers, "Cassandra."

Truth as a tiger on the road?
A literal thing, authentic, to meet or flee;
A golden fury, uprearing, constricting the brain;
With luck a fierce grappling, with scars for resistance?
A fever of conquest and a tall tale thereafter
For those who would listen, perhaps even give praise?

Come now, Cassandra, produce us this truth.
Truth is an ocean, limitless, wave upon wave,
Never ceasing, never wholly at rest,
Never fixed and at end, never plumbed.
Truth is Protean, not *the* but *a*, with a myriad faces.
Truth is a protest, a doubt, a shock, a hunch,
An urgency aimed in the dark, a wavering gleam,
A step on a slippery slope, and backward two steps,
A purging by loss, nor sudden terror nor lusting.

Jeffers, Cassandra, venting your towered pain
On the race (Cassandra, too, was locked in a tower),
Men do not always hate truth.
Mostly they grope and taste the salt of defeat;
Loath to abandon the homely cave and custom;
Lending an ear to prophets, and willing to weigh
A good proposition, but not shedding caution; not quitters;
Even in war's sewer finding equations of courage.

And if man could count on meeting truth in the road?
Would he perish of its leap and its fangs?
Would he raise fierce mandates over its carcass,
Himself becoming a flame in the narrow passage,
Showing incisors, blocking the way for late travellers,
Snarling at those more patient, more persevering?

(1948)

8

TO ONE WHO WROTE A POEM
AGAINST GRAMMAR*

SEE SYNTAX COAX in one grammatic day
More poesy than weeks of languid play;
And one fair dose of grammar's stringent purge
Release more verse than months of misty urge;
The parts of speech in neat precision seen
Provoke more rhyme than all the Freudian spleen;
While through invention runs th'electric thrill
Of grammar's bracing, prophylactic drill.

(1950)

PORTRAIT

STILL, SHE INTIMIDATED MANY. Lips
Set tight against uncalled for cosmic slips,
A tense, implastic, juiceless demoiselle,
She summoned inquisitions by her "Well!"
Her very elbows by their fingered bone
Rejected large communities alone.
Her gaunt, uncompromising granite stance
Rebuked the frivolous planets by a glance;
And common folk became with "Bah" and "Humph!"
A tiny, bitter pellet on the tongue.
How droll, to see her stiffen to her sting,
A microscopic threat to everything.

(1952, 1953)

PROFESSOR'S LAST CLASS

HE DREW A LONG HAND across a worn brow
   As if cancelling memory's stamp:
The oft-copied themes, the borrowed know-how,
   The time-saving, meagre revamp;

The compromise grade, the verbal cajole,
   Pretentious, all-promising plans;
Poor specimen fragments of learning's true whole,
   Concessions to minimum spans;

9

The pledge who copies exams for the frat,
    The friend who answers the roll;
The open notebook, the nosebleed, the brat
    Who squirms to read from his sole;

The note up the sleeve, on the nylon-clad knee,
    The smart tapping code with the shoe,
The hand-shaded eye, the clever new key
    The runs down the line with a clue;

The side-mouthing whisper, the paper held low,
    The paper held slanted, and worse;
The stretching and craning to read the next row,
    The helpful Kleenex in the purse;

The faked-indignant feminine puss,
    The grin on the vacuous mug;
Madonna-blue eyes and innocence plus,
    The surly, too muscular lug.

"Dear children," he said, and dulcet his tone,
    "One question suffices today.
Please write till you're done—I'll leave you alone—
    And cheat, by Gad, till you're gray!

"The question is this and you'd better be good—
    'My Life?'— Pass out when you're through."
He's meter-man now in a swank neighborhood,
    And sleeps as honest men do.

(c. 1950)

10

FOR WHO WILL BE I ?*

YOUNG FOLK in the classrows, scorning the opened book,
Whom do you think you hurt? Not the writers, surely;
For they by labor have earned their right of being,
While you in your nonage cling to the nurse and the mentor.

See, here sits one quite serenely, bookish to you,
But plumbing and spading around the roots of our being,
Not much at conforming, shunning expiation,
Aware of sour faces, saying what needs to be said:
Do not forever be like, glean your own ground,
To copy is but the swaddling cloth of infants;
At last one does it for oneself, or fails;
Never a man hammered a nail, plowed a new field,
Or woman bathed a new babe, measured a garment,
But made new testings each of self-reliance.

"If I am not I," said Henry, "who then will be I?"
Emily, alone in her hollyhock garden, communed
With bees and long shadows, and the tramping of hours;
Edgar, distraught, foretasted Cities of Silence;
Mad Ahab's crew set sail to pierce the mask;
And four in a boat knew deeply the color of waves;
A man on the sky accepted flame and the doubt;
And again a slow man brooded on power and the poor;
And a man on a hillside, face in the grass, savored
The oncoming of night, the ceaseless earth-swing;
And one on the shore saw dusk and its dark wings resuming;
And another probed the reticent heart of New England.

Filter them from yourself, said the good gray poet;
In the book of self you will find them, yours for the reaching;
These thoughts are yours, else they have no roots;
And free, belong to all. In time you will see it.

(1951)

11

GROSS ANATOMY
"I'll lug the guts." *Hamlet*, III, iv, 212.

THIS SLUGGISH COIL of guts (the doctor growled),
This leaky bowl, lifted on stilts and struts,
Backed with a gristly rod of concentric rings,
Stiffened with slats, and flanked with hanging claws,
Topped with a lump, a nodule sphere, stove in—
Well, there you have it; and that's the main of it.

These coils, now, call the central clamorous fact.
They're boss. Like furnaces, they must be stoked.
They're wined and dined, pampered and lugged and flushed—
Why, boy, they've marble halls and Paris gowns
Only to titillate the enteron.
You've seen 'em, planted, silk-midriffed and snug,
Nursing their goblets, scraping their greasy plates;
Or watched 'em perched in rows on cushioned seats,
Their pickers mucid with buttered corn and cokes,
Their lumpish nubbins set on osculation,
Their panting frontispieces aimed as one,
Pure glandular by proxy, on the screen.

But this nubbin, boy, this cave on rods and stilts,
Has curious spies beneath the shaggy eaves;
And shrewdly housed, too, shuttered, glassed and hinged,
Socketed, fringed—this lump takes care of its spies.
They're brain exposed—and brain's a subtle tool.
But what brain makes of their report, who knows?
I've seen 'em peer at a water-drop, a zooid,
Or study the elm-tree branches on the sky,
Or weep for strangers, none of their own; or flash
In anger at the beating of a child,
Or stare in speculation on themselves—
There may be more than guts in this, my boy.

(1953)

PART II
WAR'S ALARMS
(1918-1945)

MORNING AFTER ST. MIHIEL
(Written on the battlefield, 1918)

A LISTLESS LIGHT creeps up the East.
 The moans of wounded men,
Beaten to earth by pounding rain,
 Grope heavenward again.

But as the sun looks 'round a cloud—
 See! Heaven's neutrality:
A rainbow bridged from bleeding France
 To gaunt, gray Germany.

(1918, 1925)

AND BATTLES LONG AGO*

THE YEARS HAVE STALKED in slow procession by.
But they and all they spell can not erase
A shivered tree against the saddest sky
That ever shrouded earth; a shell-shot space
Where broken shapes in khaki blankets lie,
Some moaning in the slanting spears of rain,
Some peaceful with the peace of those who die;
Hoarse guns that crack and crash—again—again;
Lead feet that drag the length of some wet lane,
Chill streams that from the rusty helmets flow,
And sodden clothes; and dank winds that complain
And scourge the flesh, and wring the heart below.
Ah, comrades ! When the wind and sky are gray,
Far-off and long-ago seem yesterday.

(1928, 1929)

PATRIOT, 1936
("At least, the railroads in Italy run on time.")

Upon his globed and well-encushioned paunch
    He folded pudgy hands;
His belly tamed, his mind began to weave
    Its philosophic strands.

He spoke of armies, navies, flying ships,
    Accoutrements of war.
Man must be hard, alert, prepared, he said;
    He saw this more and more.

Upon the Mussolinis, Caesars stern,
    His admiration ran;
And all his grub-like fingers spread and moved
    In motion like a fan.

He'd longed, last war, to join the boys in France;
    But business was his care.
But from his private funds (inherited)
    He'd helped to get them there.

He had small use for coward youth, he said,
    Who talked and dreamed of peace;
When youth grows soft and fears to shed its blood,
    He said, the race will cease.

It was his creed that ruthless steel would put
    The masses in their place.
At that he belched and, apprehensive, stopped,
    With panic in his face.

He heaved his vast and sweaty bulk upstairs;
    He needed rest, he said;
And mumbled, "Youth must learn to love a war."
    These thoughts ran in his head.

And when at forty-six his heart, cried, "Done!"
    A chaplain took the stand,
And sobbed, "He lived four-square and firm against
    The weaklings in the land."

(1936)

15

AND ALL TO DO OVER?
(Written 1939; somewhat revised later)

AND ALL TO DO OVER, and over?
The crisis, the confabulation behind the locked doors, the
    secret resolves, the decisions made "in the name of the
    people"—
The people, the people, invariably kept in the dark, with
    little to say but much to endure;
The small men, unimportant, the men who take orders, the
    men who must go;
Mustered, transported and herded, in squads, batteries,
    regiments, by truck, in the air, but mostly plodding
    steadily afoot;
The communiques then, the claims and denials (the truth is
    not in them; headquarters lives by denials);
Then guarded admissions of first wounded, and dead, the
    somber return of the wounded, the brave new uniforms'
    slow mouldering;
The first righteous anger slow draining, the fine dedication
    turned bitter, the commitments now made realistic.

Then arise profiteering, the sly, quite legal, puffy-faced
    men,
Scrutinizers of markets, shrewd, getting while getting is
    good;
Pontifical, swivel-chair patriots, importantly phoning, confer-
    ring, traveling (expenses), stern speeches, sacrificial (of
    others), "keeping up the morale;"
The gold-braided names in the headlines, newsworthy
    names, despite a certain monotony of saying, a certain
    obtuseness of judgment;
The observant historians, with their most—almost—godlike
    detachment, prompt to determine why men should have
    died, should still go on dying;

16

The commentators, facile, all-wise, voices bland, allopathic,
full of "inside dope," and new plausibilities.
While the little men, the men without influence, offer living
flesh to stop the brute iron;
While the small men steam in the mud, lie palely in ruins, lie
sleepless in ditches, sprawl crudely on wires, lay bare the
white bone, make meals for the rats, flower in fountains
under bombing;
While at home the spate of fine words, noble, time-sacred,
tribal God-appealing words;
And pity is weakness, mercy traitorous, we must not be
human, must use the impersonal, must evade the misery
of others;
We must cover the stench, must divert the too squeamish,
reassure the too tender;
Must shout down the poets, intimidate the prophetic, pile
fagots for the reluctant, the seers of the whole in the part,
of persons as persons.

And then the roll-call of youth,
Choice fruits of the nations, plucked prematurely, aban-
doned to winds and rains and the shark's swinish tooth;
Brains, viscera, spilled on the earth, of scientists, medics,
artists, inventors, engineers, farmers and plain folk;
Of children unborn, of women unwed, the prime strength
confounded, while the unfit continue;
Of poets, Owen and Brooke, truth tellers, Siegfried Sassoon,
Barbusse, and Remarque; their thought is the same;
But their voices are wasted; the reaction sets in; the
barbarian's faith in the blood, the primitive herding,
denial of mind;
The Cain-brand ennobled, bestowed with a kiss, paraded in
streets, enamoring young women and children;
While expediency reigns; and causes no more have effects;
and the people grow callous.

Somber the clouds, the blood-lust impelling, the *revanche,*
the *Blitzkrieg;*
The rulers make faces with millions of men; the boys are
expendable, we can afford them;
Let the sky fill with iron, let wings bear the ultimate horror
and the yellow gas spread;

Women now know how flesh may be rent, is soft and will
tear; children now burrow like cubs, eat filth where they
find it;
And the people, untended, stand fronting the menace, are
shock troops for betters, are soon trampled under;
They shoulder the burden, they furnish the sons, endure the
invasions, tighten their belts, show commendable calm,
riot sometimes, but endure, they endure;
Yet flesh still quivers, the people's hearts wither, find pa-
tience a burden;
Will shrivel to indifference, or will slip into violence, will lose
their politeness and merit no mercy;
Or will one day cry out in a terrible knowledge: "And for this
we bear sons?" and "Who are the gainers?" and "Shall we
forever?"

(1939)

JUBILATE

("The High Command jubilantly announces the annihilation
of fourteen enemy divisions." AP news report, 1941)

"JUBILANT" (the very word),
    The High Command again
"Annihilates" (short wave report)
    Three hundred thousand men.
    Ju-bi-la-te, O rejoice!

Rejoice! A million pallid faces
    Blended with the mud;
Ten hundred thousand silent hearts
    Now clogged with stagnant blood.
    Ju-bi-la-te, O rejoice!

Rejoice! Not even Genghis Khan,
    Not all the great Moguls,
Could count such hosts of dead, or pile
    Such pyramids of skulls.
    Ju-bi-la-te, O rejoice!

Rejoice! and all ye lesser breeds
    Look on us and despair.
For, oh, a million empty skulls
    Have such an empty stare.
    Ju-bi-la-te, O rejoice!

Rejoice, for knowledge of all skills,
    The power of fraud and fright,
The ashes mailed, the mordant lime,
    The torture in the night.
    Ju-bi-la-te, O rejoice!

Rejoice! Rejoice! The High Command
    Proclaims the road to peace:
Lie, starve, and kill, and jubilant,
    Mark how the dead increase.
    Ju-bi-la-te, O rejoice!

(1941)

19

MARS SAITH TO YOUNG POETS

Go SONGLESS toward the dark;
    No rhymed and metered moan.
By rigid reticence
    Be uniformly known.

Cry halt, the eager pen,
    Cry hold, the fledgling flight.
Guard well the burning word
    That starts up in the night.

Eyes front, obey this hour,
    Its iron charge, its wrath.
Fall in and, voiceless, march
    Along the shadowed path.

(1941, 1944)

PRIVATE FIRST CLASS: 1944

WORD TO MY PARENTS, friends:
    This day I came of age,
And signalized my twenty-first
    In forced and shameful rage.

For fifty men I sped to death
    By murderous short-range fire,
By skillful twistings of the blade,
    By faces in the mire.

Prepare your favored formula,
    Arrange your mouldy spell,
Oh, exorcise this curse of Cain,
    For I have tasted hell.

Nor can I promise to abstain,
    Nor have I pause for sorrow,
For now a hundred hunt revenge,
    And we hunt them tomorrow.

(1944, 1948)

20

CHILD, MAN, AND WATCHER*

INSISTENT SIRENS on the London night
Rush folk in half-dressed haste beneath the streets;
Resignedly, the commonweal retreats
And disciplines the rawness of its flight.

Observe the media of self-control,
The pregnant forms that craft and courage take:
Though some may sleep, the most, for honor's sake,
Must test the dark resources of the mole.

Here children's brief, unbrooding memories
Find concentration in a fragile game;
Here lovers fan the duocentric flame,
Withdrawn in their discrete parentheses.

And mother care, and priestly grace, disguise
Their private hurt by tending others' fear;
Doctor and nurse unpack their nerveless gear
And rally flesh with swift, impartial eyes.

But ah, the watcher on the shattered night
Faces a harsh, uncharitable sky;
The city cowers in a bitter light,
Naked beneath the old, relentless "Why?"
There is a courage which, though weaponless,
Must share the shame and still not acquiesce.

(1945)

WOUNDED

POOR BODY, now unveiled,
Palely entreats, "Has Death yet won—
Or failed?"

(1970)

21

PART III
OF WYOMING
(1934-1948)

ABANDONED MINING CAMP *

I

THE GRAY ROCK-RIM, shining with patches of snow, bulks
    firm, incisive, upon the limpid blue.
And the evergreens, how dark and solid they flow,
Striding long slopes, encompassing this narrow gorge.
How uneventful here in the summer sun these faded paths,
Where grasses bend beside a stripling brook;
These three gray cabins, this slab-sided engine shed,
The rusty boiler within, humping its riveted hoops at the
    roof,
And the cable, groping its sterile strand down the dark hole.
The sun weaves patterns upon the drunken floor, the cob-
    webs cluster on the beams;
The trees bend motionless upon the brook, wrapped in
    waves of the sun;
The wind sighs lazily around the eaves, fingering the fringes
    of pine;
And the aspens whisper drowsily together.

II

Sedately the autumn raindrops plash on the roof;
The first tattoo, the slow, delaying, ponderous rhythm; and
    then the impetuous rush.
The gray sky rests on the hill; the mist settles damply upon
    the ridge,
The clouds drag tenuous veils across the pines,
And wisps of spray cling to the clotted-wet mountain grass.
The valley is enclosed, remote, a place forgot, abandoned to
    the sky and its waters.
Three dark doorways gape in the slanting rush,
The swift rain-rush, drumming on the dingy pane, washing
    the walls.
Three roofs sag lower, sodden with moss and mud,
Rotting to feed the insatiable valley grass.

III

The thin-edged winter winds sweep down from the pass.
The withered grass rustles and stiffens; the fine snow
    streams aslant.
Three cabins and a shed stand cowering in the blast,
And within, the rusted levers chatter feebly.

The black wells up from the shaft, and no echo is there.
The brittle snow pelts on the walls and the windows, tiny,
    insistent,
Edging in at a hundred cracks and crannies,
Thrusting hard at the last crazed door.
And then, on the pallid margin of the night,
Cold shadows waver, and grow gray, and the hinges com-
    plain;
The snow whips inside, and hurries across the splintered
    floor;
And soundless in the empty corners, the darkness crouches.

(1934)

DECEMBER FRAGMENT

AMONG THE PYRAMIDAL PINE
He halted his shuffling, snow-shoe gait
And squinted upward, wrinkling at the points of white
That sped, infinite to count, like broken spray,
Straight for his face, out of his private, close-gathering sky.
Beside him here, among the trees, a few flakes drifted,
Hovering like feathers, idly floating above the curved pagoda
    branches.
White and dusky green, these were the only colors of the
    world,
As on he pushed, in broad, splay-footed, whispering splashes.

    Until here, at the edge of the wood,
A million needle-sharpened spears sprang pricking at his
    cheek;
A mad snow-dust streamed over the granite humps, or
    spiralled around the stiff sage-brush;
And all was rushing winds, and patches stripped bare by the
    wind, and then the eyeless, fleeting gray.
Tugging at his belt, feeling the wind in his teeth, his voice
    thrust back in his throat,
He hunched a shoulder at the gale, sideways glancing at the
    windblown waste;
And bowing to the storm, he labored up the slope,
And was drawn into the wild, night brooding sky.

The sky dimming to dark with the hours,
Clearing with the moon, paraded its myriad frosty stars.
The earth lay faintly gleaming, the white world dimly shin-
    ing; the air hung taut with cold;
The hills, black limned in the west, breathless in the steely
    chill,
Loomed vast and impassive against the icy-spangled sky.

And he, solitary pausing on a barren knoll,
Long looking at the hills, and the mountains' clean-edged
    line,
The sky, and the stars, and the wide-lying snow,
Turned last to a tiny light that winked in the lap of the
    darkest slope;
Then thrice he threshed his arms about him, slow breathing
    from his tired ribs;
And eagerly the wide-webbed feet went whispering down
    the hill.

(1937, 1941)

SHEEPHERDER'S WIND *

AGAIN, IN THE DARKNESS,
Whole cavalcades of wind, rushing through Wyoming's
    midnight sky;
Battalions, legions, that pushed preoccupied, intent,
Across the high, thin acreage of the sky, above the shoulder-
    ing ridges,
On continental errands, Saskatchewan to Mexico;
To some austere accounting,
To some fierce council-spot of all the winds of earth,
Ice-starkness of Alaskan heights, and upper Andean peaks,
Wyoming but the thoroughfare.

The solitary man, the sheepherder,
His mind, as happened now, bent on his single thought,
A trifle shy on certitudes, because of many solitary days and
    nights,
Measured off his dusty patch of ground beneath his wagon's
    arch,

Set leeward of a bare outcrop of rock,
With thirty miles of sage-brush land, east and west, between
    the brooding peaks;
And laid him down, pondering long upon the wind;
As if its roar had not already flooded all his brain with empty
    sound,
As if it had not swept and polished the very corners of his
    mind.

    He knew the old jack-rabbit, crouched beneath his
        shaggy sage-brush stem,
His ears laid flat, his belly tense, his back fur ruffled into tips
By the tags of wind that sniffed along the ground;
He knew the gopher, sitting with apprehensive snout at his
    dark door,
His eyes like brittle beads;
He knew the windblown stars, and saw their streamers
Churned across the dishevelled night.

    But more surely, more inwardly, he knew—
Hearkening, thinking long upon the wind,
Gripped by the one sure thing Wyoming nights of wind had
    taught him—
Knew firmly that they three,
The old jack-rabbit, cowered beneath the wan-green sage-
    brush leaves,
The gopher, taut, unblinking at his labyrinth's black door,
The herdsman, aging sinews curled about the sage-brush
    roots—
That they three could in no way be
Concern of winds like these.

                                (1937,1938)

ON A NAKED HILL IN WYOMING*

On a naked hill in Wyoming,
Mike Phillipoulos from Macedonia, lying under the thin
    gravelly sod,
And next him Pavlovitch from Serbia, the wooden cross
    slanting;
And others, miners of coal. For accidents will always be.
And Maria Pinelli, aged three, dead of a fever,
The mother gone now to Napoli,
That last day scrawling across the granite stone,
In shaken pencilled letters, half blurred even now by the
    wind and the rain,
O carissima mia, addio.

The dark forested hills of Dakota face westward,
Backing the naked hill, the low promontory,
Looking sunward on leagues of gaunt, marginal land,
With strange buttes rising, apart, far distant, mysterious,
Against the glistening afternoon sky,
Like great ship-bulks, forever stranded on a static sea;
And the graveyard lying lonely on the stark headlands.

Three miles going on the crisp short grass, the landscape
    gently tipping,
And there the abrupt pause, the ugly gash yawning;
The hundred rotting wooden steps, lurching down the steep,
    grassy side,
The rusted rails, the tottering trestles,
The empty shafts, like a throat that's been slit,
The chute, black-clotted with dust,
The lateral gorges, the streets reclaimed by the swift-running
    streams,
The houses, now bowing to earth,
The hollow, echoing hotel, the boss' big house;
And the bird within, beating vain wings upon the window
    pane.

Phillipoulos of Macedonia, Pavlovitch, Kronstadt, the
    others,
Meagerly entrenched against Time and his gnawing,
Under the simple stone and the anonymous grass they lie,
Peripheral sparks, flung off by the forges of trade;
Spent spray from the whirlpools of commerce, the long tra-
    jectory ended.

And *O carissima mia, addio,*
Fading in the sun, on a naked hill in Wyoming.

(1938, 1939)

FOREWORD TO WYOMING

COME, LET US CONSIDER firsts in Wyoming.
Here, we are new, our roots are not yet deep.
"Only yesterday," the aged will say, "And we still living re-
    member..."
And folding withered hands they muse, and these the vin-
    tage of their days:
The Oregon Trail, Jim Bridger, Washakie, Buffalo Bill;
The old fort, the ranch, the first white child, the last buffalo
    herd;
The great blizzard, the laying of rails, the crude bar, the tree-
    less frame town.

"Powder River!" men cry, a wild surge in their throats.
For this is the land of the few against the unpersonal much;
Of uncommunicative spaces and stoic horizons, and the con-
    sciousness of holding on;
The newness of nostrils tingling to the untamed scent of
    sagebrush after rain;
Of a roving Spaniard, pausing at the edge, gazing northward
    on the Rio Verde;
Of a voyageur, shading wondering eyes on the Black Hills
    and the Montagnes Rocheaux;
Of lone mountain men, proving the Wind River Canyon, the
    Medicine Bow, Twogwotee Pass, and the lakes by the
    Tetons;
Of the first small bands, naming the Belle Fourche, the
    Chugwater, the Poison Spider.

And before them, the Indians, filtering into the valleys:
Blackfeet and Sioux, the Cheyenne, the Shoshoni, Flathead
      and Nez Perces;
Out of what impenetrable past? And with what names before
      the white naming?
Making songs of the rivers, the Popo Agie, the Seeds-ke-dee
      Agie and the Niobrara.
But their first are not known: what councils they held in cold
      winters;
What wisdom was theirs of buffalo haunts and rare hunting,
      caves and hot waters;
When first they circled stone rings, or gathered the rock for
      the arrow and the great wheel;
Or painted with red berry stains; or carved the petroglyph on
      the deep canyon wall.

This is a new land, a story soon told...
But here in my hand, an egg-shaped, dull, glistering object;
Gastrolith; stomach-stone of old monsters, polished by juices,
      incredibly ancient.
And how shall we date these phantom feeders?
How envisage them, gorging on tropical green, here in Wyo-
      ming?
Stretching grotesquely long necks for matted marsh food;
      gobbling down pebbles for grinding;
Trapped by their weight in the slime, helpless, floundering,
Sluggish limbs caught, leaving huge bone-frames to prove
      them?

This is new land, but newly known...
Yet here on a great space of short grass, centered in silence,
The summer sun brooding, the deep summer sky endlessly
      breathless,
There lies extended a tree, stone tree, perdurable stone.
And who will upraise it, and show it intact and alive?
Did it tower by some palm-scented sea a million, ten million
      time-counts ago?
Did it bend by a lake, before quadrupeds ventured to
      browse?
Did it cast its long shadow on some undiscoverable stream ?

Firsts in Wyoming are strange beyond counting, out of
    man's listing.
Seas lipped at old shores; shores shrugged off the waters;
    landscapes folded in patterns;
Mountains sank into plains; plains rose, and were sky-reach-
    ing;
Centuries labored; fierce sunshine and rain, frost, wind and
    earth-weight persevered;
Shaping earth's tegument, fashioning climate and soil;
Finding room for odd creatures, Triceratops, Tyrannosaurus,
    Eohippus;
Dissolving these; giving place to new forms, more familiar;
The shrill coney, the grizzly, the white-tufted antelope;
Accepting proud man in due time, the red man, the white;
Molding each kind of life in its turn; molding us.

(1944, 1945)

MOUNTAIN BRAND
(A Parable)

"MOUNTAINS WILL PUT their brand upon a man."
Jeff puffed his pipe of reminiscing leisure.
He'd lots of time. A ranch in winter days
Isn't an eastern farm—no woodlot work,
No ice to harvest, hours when one can pause.
    "'Tisn't so much that each man's *for* himself—
You tend to share your findings in the open—
As that so often he's just *by* himself,
To learn the hard way what a lone man's worth.
You have no crowd-like minds to hide behind;
And not much point to say society's
The sole excuse for any fellow's folly;
No unions, to pretend that each man's worth
Comes out the same. And somehow, too, a man
Had better watch his claim to being boss;
Even your horse might challenge that someday.
You have your freedom, but it's not by rights.
It's something earned, something you prove you have.

Plucking a thread from Time's capricious weave,
Jeff smiled, "Wind River country, there's a place
I flourish in. Minds me of one pack trip—
And Doctor Steiff, a dentist from Detroit,
His first time West, and last time, too, I guess.
Party of eight we were, including guide.
Well sir, we'd packed as much as several days
From any town, and towns are scarce ther'bouts.
This Steiff was man enough, a hefty chap,
For all his city ways. He'd watch me close,
Polite, you'd say, and taking notes to learn;
A bit too smooth in speech, perhaps; and then
Some little signs of temper ill-controlled.
    "I noted smallish things at first—the way
He kicked a horse; and how his face went hard
When I called out at him; and how he thought
My contract called for me to be his guide
The livelong day. The others found their way.
I'd leave him fishing—go to check on things—
And he would glare as if I'd broke corral.
And then in camp, how much he liked to argue:
How times had changed, how men no longer hold
By outworn themes, like individual rights.
There was a sort of hard-bit logic to it,
Except he always brought around to prove
That *he* was somehow thereby made to rule.
    " 'But that ain't mountain sense,' I stuck in once,
'The freer each man is, the freer all.'
'Mountains!' he sneered. 'The home of backwash ways.'
I let it pass, although my hackles rose,
Especially as he treated my two bits
As if some servant spoke it out of turn.
'But we are individuals here, at least,'
One party said. 'That's why I'm here, I think,
To get away from pressures on the Self,
To find a spot where elemental things
Are clarified.' 'That's nonsense,' Steiff would say;
'The elemental law is Strong rule Weak.
I'm here to build my strength. The weak go under.'

32

"It happened sudden as a mountain squall.
I might have guessed that he'd be panic-stung,
But still hard-mouthed, and ornery as a burro.
Evening was coming on, and I was casting
About for some right place to camp, but feeling
The peace of mountain quiet on my spirits,
Knowing we'd still a couple of days to go,
When up comes Steiff, half worried, half a kind
Of arrogance. 'You there!' he says, 'You guide!
Do you know where we are? Sure you're not lost?
By Himmel, I think you plan to lose us here!
Something is wrong, and I'm not one to stand
One side and let some dumb subordinate
Make rules for me. You, guide, where are we now?'

    "Well, sir, I've seen 'em loco in the hills,
There's women gets a kind of all-lost state,
And have to stick to me like cockle-burrs.
But this was something new; it nettled me.
'Wind River Mountains ain't so far,' I say.
'Come!' says he. 'None of your subterfuges now.
I watched you standing there, a moment back,
Staring around. You've lost your bearings, guide!
Don't try to hide the obvious from me.
A strong hand comes to be necessity
In times like this.'

                    "By then I saw the man
Was hardly like himself, or else too like.
He wouldn't wait. 'What is that mountain called?
This map I have—it doesn't show a lake.'
'Don't know,' I says. 'They've never had a name—'
'So that's the trick ! I thought as much. You're lost !'
'Now, Mr. Steiff—' 'Doctor to you,' he snaps.
The others gathered 'round. He made a speech.
'I'm taking charge,' he says. 'This fellow's lost.
We'll leave at once,' he screams. 'You'll follow me !'
And two or three began to hesitate,
Especially as I never said a word—
A lad from Omaha, a man from Portland,
And one from Buffalo, New York. They rolled
Their eyes like stallions smelling too much smoke;

33

And off they went, by gad, over a ridge
To find a valley like to mine as peas,
Only a step the other way from home.
There wasn't a one had packed in there before.
     "I let them go. My wrangler Shorty winked
But kept a solemn face. I looked at Ford,
A silent chap, who'd stand and gaze at streams
As if he'd found what he'd been missing long;
New to the range, but calm. and no one's fool.
'You're sticking, then.' I says, not asking, though.
'I hadn't heard you call for help,' he smiled.
Then there's a lad from Tennessee quite keen.
'Well, lad,' I said, noting his eager eyes,
You'd better trail that maverick stampede.
Keep out of sight. You'll find us camped down stream.'
     "The air was getting crisp. The peaks had pulled
Their twilight cloaks about their chests, and stars
Began to advertise for frosty nights,
Before the boy came back, his face a-grin
At playing scout. 'I followed them,' he says.
'They're rim-rocked, camping on an open slope,
And shivering in the wind; no water close.
They've built a monster fire, and placed a guard.
I guess they think the Indians or bears
Will creep up on them, if they don't set watch.'
     "Well, sir, we spent the next day out of sight,
Letting them wander until almost dark.
They'd crossed one ridge, and then another, hoping
To 'orient' themselves. But peaks begin
To look alike and strange, and rocks repeat;
And when my lad came strolling, casual-like,
Trout in his creel, and fishing rod in hand,
And hailed them in surprise, they almost wept.
'You came to find us after all,' said Steiff.
'To find you? Why, I thought you'd headed home.
We're pulling out tomorrow,' says the lad.
'Not leaving us! No, please! You can't do that!
Somehow we can't find any roads or paths.'
'Good reason why. There are no paths to find.
All right. If that's the case, just tag along.

I guess old Jeff can pick his way to town.'
    "The lad was boy enough to have his say.
'Jeff still can't name that lake, but that's because
It never had a name. Most mountain men
Have had to learn to read their mountains straight.
And how did you imagine maps were made?
Besides, you always have to compromise,
Some trial and error, else we'd never grasp
Even enough to keep what others knew,
Much less leave room for changes yet to come.'
    "But Steiff was one of those who never learn.
He stalked in like some corporal on parade.
'You win,' he says, stiff as a dentist's drill;
'You give the orders now, and I obey.'
    "But that's not mountain sense, this boss and slave.
Mountains aren't made for mobs or slaves, I hold.
Mountains aren't evil spirits—nor goods ones, either.
They're nature's ways; and man, to get along,
Has got to fit himself into their habits.
'Certain inalienable rights'—I guess
That means the right to learn from bottom up
Your own best way, and take the consequence."
    Jeff rose and knocked the ashes from his pipe.
"Called me a dumb subordinate, the fool.
Maybe that's why I recollect this Steiff.
And yet I sorta hoped he'd take to mountains,
Perhaps come back another year and brush
The crazy cobwebs off his brain. . . You know,
I can't quite like to see his kind increase. . .
Maybe my name ain't Jefferson for nothing."

(1944)

CONTINENTAL DIVIDE*

"Look!" he called sharply, "Look!" his head half turned,
His fishing rod extended for a pointer,
His footing firm. his body taut and eager,
His face alight at being first to see;
His voice the voice you use when you've discovered
A rarity, an Indian tomahawk,
A deep-marsh bloom, and eagle brought to earth;
"Look here! Here's something you won't often see,"
    Coming along, I stared, not certain what
To fix upon. I saw a tiny stream,
Hardly a full-length step from bank to bank;
Some sturdy, spiralled pines near timberline,
Their needles sparsely strewn on rock-ribbed soil;
Sparse grasses nervous in the fresh, high breeze;
And water spilling from the sills and eaves
Of snowbanks piled roof-like on the summits;
Or, hushed with distance, lower gorges threading
Pine-purple hills and humps and lesser shoulders;
The always moving vista of these heights,
And space—and space—and still the spacious sky.
    "Come, use your eyes! Here's something you won't see
From here to Timbuctoo!" Impatiently
His rod tip nudged the little hurrying rill.
    The water chuckled low. It played around
A little point of land, a dark earth-wedge
That split the stream. Waters divided here—
Divided here! The laggard mind drew breath.
And opened wide to take a continent in:
This was the spot—the watershed, the ridge,
The earth-sphere line of all America;
Busily separating right from left,
While we looked on. And this way East, the Platte,
Missouri, Mississippi, no way back;
And that way West, the Little Snake, the Yampa,
The Green, the Colorado's mighty ditch.
This drop Atlantic bound; this fellow drop
Pacific drawn—and here before our eyes. . .

The eastward tumbling gorge, the westward slope—
There was no doubt—and each forever leaving
The continental vertebra behind.

We turned once more to mark the very spot.
A wavering weed inclined, antenna-like,
Restlessly touching, bouncing on the stream,
As if to gauge the line invisible.
We scratched it twenty feet behind the wedge
And drew it on the air, and stood perplexed.

The waters gushed beneath an eastern bank
But, thrust athwart the slope by some low bulge,
They veered and crossed this lower saddle-back—
Or almost crossed, for here the subtle law
Had caught and held the balance for a fraction,
And set the imperceptible divide.

The imperceptible divide—though still
Perceptible enough in consequence.
And yet the line, from land's end arrow point
To western bank, and how it worked to part
The waters here, just here, and nowhere else.
Eluded. Mind was sure, and yet unsure.
East, West, the signs we know. Yet here to shave
The line to less than hairbreadth subtlety...
Line is a length, nor breadth nor thickness found,
And point is less, and has position only.
Extent and parts unknown; and all is south,
If we but measure from the northern pole.
These are the facts serene, and these the proofs.
And yet—and yet—how firm and sure the line,
How wide the ways, how far apart the drops
That rushed upon their swift decision here.

Silently standing, each pursued his thought;
And he, constant in fealty to his faith,
Extracting fresh allegiance and a moral;
And I, content with earth's abundant uses,
And earth's clean workshop ways, and hills and skies.

"I'll take the West," he said. "The way is farther,
But there are lakes I'd like to try once more;
Besides, the West has much the longer view.
I'll have the bigger fish, and maybe more."
"And I the Eastern Way," I said at last.

37

"The pools are not so far apart, and though
I may not be the fisherman you are,
I'll show some catch, perhaps my limit, too."
    We smiled, acknowledging the hidden theme,
Another sort of unseen, parting line,
With ways that branched. For him the ancient "call,"
For me empiric, present urgencies.
For him no compromise, despite my saying
That at the distant pole all ways converge,
And there the deepest oceans blend, and there
No line is found.

(1945, 1946)

LARAMIE HILLS *

THE RAW WIND RUNS the hills like icy flame;
    Long slopes of sage lie low;
The lonely cedar hugs the granite rock
    And bows in scuds of snow.
Along the gray outcrop, against the wind
    Leaning, I move alone,
And mark the briar's scant and withered tune
    Upon the faceless stone.
The frozen aspens group within the draw;
    Forlornly hangs the leaf;
Who pastures high will feed on slender fare,
    Austere and tough and brief.

Incredibly, the dun-limbed antlered buck,
    Unmoved in his retreat,
Merges within the mottled aspen boles,
    Snow dunes about his feet.
What catalyst compounds this crushed-sage scent,
    This dwarfed and fibered tree?
What rock-roomed distillation searches out
    The cedar's chemistry?
How came the buck, breathing the mantling snow,
    Wide-pronged and proud to see;
Confronting thus this high, reluctant land,
    This chill frugality?

(1946, 1946)

38

SOUTH-SOUTHWESTWARD GAZING

FORTH FROM THIS BRIEF OASIS, Laramie town,
Forth from the office window, the eye with what satisfaction
    assenting,
Skimming the treeless plain, south-southwestward digress-
    ing,
Boulder Ridge and the Sand Creek dip, the Poudre and the
    Rabbit Ear Pass,
No visible hut or hamlet between, a few faint trails disre-
    garded—
Such, indeed, one muses, is the general prospect,
Pin-point and line on the map concurring,
From here to the Golfo de California and the Mexican moun-
    tains,
A thousand miles unimpeded, no less, swift swept by the
    wingless vision.
    Thus out of the window gazing, the mind's eye unop-
    posed errant,
Saluting the Medicine Bow, the Never Summer and the
    Mummy Ranges,
The snow-shining crests and crags of the Rockies,
The pine-dusk Uncompaghre, the Mesa Verde and the an-
    cient cliffs,
The Navajo country and the Hopi, the Canyon's great gash,
The painted Desert, the Laguna Salada,
The rainless sands and the Golfo and the bone-bare Mexican
    wastes—
    Well, it's tonic to think on a land unsubdued, where few
    wish to loiter:
A prospector, perhaps, bemused; some soldier-corps cursing;
    a few scurrying tourists;
A few Indians resolutely surviving; an eagle high soaring...
And thus, too, to have slipped away oneself, by a peopleless
    route,
To have been vagrant, unnoted, from duty, and that old ro-
    dent, Time;
To have made no commitments.

                                     (1946)

SKY OVER 'BIG HOLLOW'

Even the autumn cloud-drift brushed with bronze and
gold,
And through the pass three farthest peaks, last signalling
light;
Even the day withdrawing, olive-pale, not cold;
And even so, the slow, impalpable increase of night.

(1947, 1949)

WE, BORNE ALONG*

The western light withdraws, retreats; the hills face
westward and wait;
The cool night-stars emerge, confirmers of space, in clusters,
or shining apart;
The great granite boulders draw closer, dark, heavy; the
aspens pause in their whispering;
The evening breeze rests; there is no sound.

The east now is glowing, dimly suffused, the sun's moon-
mirror is coming,
The ghost of daytime, following on day, the revenant, mak-
ing familiar unfamiliar;
And the eastern ridge is a bar against light, a barrier opposing
the glow;
And duskily etched, remote, a lone pine is lifted, signaler,
apprizer,
A measurer of moons, awaiting the comer.

Look! the yellow dim-disc is rising; and the pine is an
arrow, its shaft
Feathered, obscuring; then cleaving the golden gong; then a
hand on a dial, saying twelve;
And almost one catches the pine-point's time-clocking, the
up-going, the moon's progress measured
The silent, conjunctive spheres, the balance of planets.

But hold! It is earth, our earth, that so spins; and we,
borne along, are in motion;

40

And the pine finger drifts like a pilot's rod at the prow,
    stately in pace by the cliff,
The horizon rising as the ship comes to harbor, as the hill-
    circled harbor comes forward;
Old earth gliding on its elder, swift track, heaving on its keel
    toward the disc,
    Its pine prow dipping, like a mast on a deck.

For earth-ball is pressing around on its course, steadily
    pivoting eastward;
And we, the passengers, on its dervish bulk whirling,we are
    forever unheedful;
But the lone pine announces it, timing, reminding, then
    dropping below the moon-dial,
    Ready for the sun, and the morning star.

And we the forgetful, assuming all fixed, unable to hold
    to the fact,
Repeat the old myth of Dian, and of moon's motion, and of
    rising and setting of suns...
And behind us the granite is glittering with crystals of mica,
    winking and twinkling,
Till the boulders seem buoyant like massy balloons, hardly
    anchored in the golden-dim mist,
Hardly freighting this moon-struck globe, this earth.

                         (1947. 1948)

ANTELOPE CREEK*

TAKE TIME FOR FAR HORIZONS, stretch the eye
For tranquil largeness, prodigal, remote;
Measure by sky and distant slanted showers,
Cool shadows, languid on the buttes, slow hawks,
The small occasional flash of antelope rumps;
A distant drifting speck, a man on horse,
Threading the nameless rims and naked knolls
On silent hooves, soundless upon a bluff,
Ancestral unit, mounted, isolate,
Like something lost in ways half mythical.

Think with that horseman lost in pathless grass,
Moving in silence, microscopic, lone,
Passing beyond, unnamed, casual in space—
Does he reflect: This older way is best?
The slow, firm earth, the rims, the grassy hollow,
And I here, unmolested, taste my days;
With time to pace the rhythm of the skies,
And sun, and elemental vagrant winds?

More likely, jogging on, not wasting words,
He hides a hard attachment and a bent
For elbow room and space. Crooking his knee
About the saddle horn, he shifts his weight,
Sways lightly on, considers food and drouth,
And where to bed, and where his cattle graze.

(1948, 1949)

PART IV
OF FOREIGN TONGUES
(1923-1969)

NOTE ON UNTRANSLATABLES

The classic, the near-perfect poem, resists total translation. The perfect music, the blend of vowel and consonant, overtones of connotation, nuances of words in context, are lost. A literal prose sacrifices rhythm; a verse translation juggles for rhyme and a semblance of form.

The two poems below, the one an anonymous French poem, the other by the German Goethe, will illustrate. The French is classic in its cool anonymity, its decorum, its abstract statement, its quality of the Greek anthology or the Latin epigram, its tone of acceptance, even its mathematical balance of 5, 4, 5, 4 syllables and the identical number of letters for each stanza. It must be dimeter and tetrasyllabic in English, yet "a little" will not do for repeated wording. One has to supply words in excess of the original. The German, in contrast, is romantic, in its detail from nature, its personal note, its freedom in form, its "sensibility." No substitute rhymes are quite adequate.

So, with apologies:

French

LA VIE est vaine:	AH, LIFE is vain:
Un peu d'amour,	A love, a song,
Un peu de haine,	A hate, a pain,
Et puis, bon jour.	And then, so long.
La vie est brève:	Ah, life is brief:
Un peu d'espoir,	A hope, a sigh,
Un peu de rêve,	A dream, a grief,
Et puis, bon soir.	And then, good-bye.

German

ÜBER ALLEN Gipfeln	ON ALL the mountain tops
Ist Ruh,	Is peace,
In allen Wipfeln	In every wood and copse
Spürest du	Winds cease;
Kaum einen Hauch:	Scarcely a breeze.
Die Vögelein schweigen	Small birds are silent on the nest.
im Walde.	
Warte nur! Balde	Wait. Soon thou like these
Ruhest du auch.	Shalt rest.

(1968)

THE BLACKSMITHS *

(Note: Early English, 14th century, alliterative four-beat measure, old as *Beowulf* and echoed in some Mother Goose rhymes, as "Little Tommy Tucker, Sang for his supper." Here it imitates the hammer on the anvil.)

SWART AND SOOTY blacksmiths smoke-stained and splattered,
Drive a man to death's door dinging at their cling-clang.
Noise they make at night-time never man endured it:
Shouts and shrieks of servants, screams and knocks and crashes;
Crooked-featured cullions crying loud for "Coal! Coal!"
Blowing at their bellows enough to burst their brains out:
"Huf, puf!" from this one "Haf, paf!" another one.
Sprawling, spitting workmen sputtering their jargon,
Grind and grate and bellow groaning all together.
Sweltering and sweating at the strong, hard hammering.
Beaten from a bull's hide be their leathern aprons;
Sheaths upon their shanks to shield them from the fire-sparks.
Heavy hammers wield they that hard be to handle.
Stiff strokes strike they upon the sturdy anvil:
Lus, bus! Las, das! loudly each in his turn.
Dolesome the din, may the devil drive it from us!
The master takes a small piece pounds upon a petty one,
Twists the twain together strikes a merry treble:
Tic, tak! hic, hac! tiket, taket, tik, tak!
Lus, bus! Lus, das, such a life they lead me!
Who can rest at night-time for hissing of the waters?
Harness-making mare's men Christ make them sorrow!

(1931)

THE TOMB OF EDGAR POE*
(From Mallarmé sonnet, "Le Tombeau d'Edgar Poe.")

THE POET, changed by Time into his own,
With naked sword inflames a startled age,
Aghast to know that it misprized his page,
His strange, wild voice, in death prodigious grown.

When to the tribes the purer word is shown,
Upstart, the Hydra-headed heathen rage;
So lesser men proclaimed his beverage
Black witches' brew from shameless floods and lone.

If out of hostile earth and sky, O grief,
Our thought can work to carve no bas-relief
Worthy to mark the dazzling tomb of Poe
(Calm block here fallen from ill-starred events),
At least this granite shall forever show
The bounds to Blasphemy's black insolence.

(1936, 1942)

*See Addenda for French sonnet.

CRÉPUSCULE SUR WYOMING
(Translation of "Sky Over Big Hollow." p. 40)

LÀ-BAS, des lambeaux de nuages de l'automne, teintés d'or et
de bronze,
Et à travers le col, trois pics qui signallent de loin un jour en
retraite;
Et maintenant le ciel qui se retire, pâle et frais et couleur de
l'olive;
Et ainsi la marche soutenue, ininterrompue, implacable, de la
nuit.

(1955)

MORCEAUX   FRAGMENTA
(Written in French, then Englished)

LES TÂCHES quotidiennes
  S´imposent;
Peu à peu deviennent
  Tout ce qu´on ose.
	THE COMMON daily task
	  Ensnares;
	Too soon becomes quite all
	  One dares.

Les mythes t´accordent grand confort;
  Les jours sont durs sans eux.
Laisse dire un homme la vérité,
  Le tout devient douteux.
	Fictions, myths, they comfort us;
	  Life would be hard without.
	But let a man advance a truth,
	  And all is thrown in doubt.

Partout les trop croyants
  S´occupent,
Soit partisans brûlants,
  Soit dupes.
	Behold the true believers
	  In troops,
	As ardent partisans,
	  As dupes.

Qui doit tout affronter, comment,
  Pourquoi?
L´être vivant, se trouvant là,
  Le moi.
	Who questions all, the how, the what
	  The why?
	The living being, being there,
	  The I.

Pas de musique dans le luth
  Si on manque la tension;
La corde lâche, sourde et brute,
  Mérite aucune attention.
	No music dwells within the string
	  If lack there be of tension;
	Slack or sagging will not sing,
	  Nor merit aught of mention.

Ce sont les longues années
  Qui savent
Que les choses trop gaies
  Sont graves.
	By means of lengthened years
	  We learn
	What once had seemed delight
	  May burn.

Ainsi va la vie, je sais.
  Que faire?
Poliment dire que oui, et
  Se taire.
	So go our lives, I know.
	  Therefore?
	Politely say, ah yes, and so
	  No more.

(c.1970)

CRÉPUSCULAIRE	TWILIGHT
Crépuscule.	The twilight falls
Tout recule.	On hills and halls.
Lumière?	With fading light
Fragmentaire.	Comes waning sight.
Bougie crève	The candle's beam
Dans un rêve.	Is as a dream.
Le jour conquis,	When that shall fail,
Vient la nuit.	Night will prevail;
Quand tout se tait,	At which surcease
Vient la paix.	There cometh peace;
Viens et dure,	A peace so pure,
Paix si pure.	May it endure.

(1971)

BODY *
(From the *Journal* of Paul Valéry, "Ton Corps," a fragment)

THOUGH I FORGET, body will never be far away.
Though I felt nothing, body had shifted still.
I talk, but body it is that will act.
I see, but body itself is blind.
I walk, and body trudges along.
I taste; body accepts and digests.
I smile; all body can do is wrinkle.
I sleep; body sleeps.
Body never knew how I sifted my thoughts;
Nor I how body, deep down, was making perforce its changes.

(1960, 1969)

BE SILENT *
(From Paul Valéry, "Tais-toi.")

HERE IS an excellent title...
An excellent sum of the whole...
　　Surpassing an "opus"...
And yet—an opus:—"For"
　　If you enumerate—each of the occasions
when the form and the movement
of a word, like a wave,
swells, and defines itself—
　　Beginning with a sensation,
a surprise, a remembrance,
a presence or an emptiness...
a good, an evil—a nothing and a Whole,
　　And if you but observe, if you seek,
if you feel, and weigh
the means to oppose this dominion,
the weight of weights to put on your tongue
and the trial of restraint on your will,
　　You will know wisdom and power
and to *Be Silent* will be more beautiful
than the hosts of smiles and the rivulets of pearls
whereof the mouth of man is most lavish.

(1964, 1967)

POEM WITHOUT TITLE
(Adapted from Raymond Queneau, "Untitled Poem.")

DEAF IS THE NIGHT, and the mist,
The pebble is deaf, and the tree,
Deaf is the hammer, the wrist,
The owl is deaf, and the sea.

Blind is the night, and the stone,
Blind is the grass, the corn.
Blind is the mole, alone,
Blind the fruit, and the thorn.

Mute is the night, and the pain,
Mute the song, and the air,
Mute is the wood, and the rain,
The lake, the cry of despair.

Feeble is nature, unsure,
Feeble the beasts, and the rocks,
Feeble the caricature,
Feeble the fool when he mocks.

Who then will hear, speak, see?

(1967)

PART V
TIMES OF LOSS
(1944-1969)

PARENTS *

PARENTS ABIDE like seasoned trees
    To reassure the eye;
Though gnarled and bent, by custom still
    Between us and the sky.

But when they drop to earth's cool couch,
    Such space invades, we know
That we in turn front silent stars
    And shield yet others so.

(1944)

TRUCE

INFLECT THE END tips toward the palm,
    Make slack the agent hand,
Night-cloud the subtle spheres
    Beneath the temple's band.

Wrap silken husks about the form
    Whose pliant pipes are spent,
Unwind the net upon whose threads
    The messages once went.

So endeth errant this brief flight,
    This patient pulse hath ceased.
Now lieth captious flesh, apart,
    Preoccupied, released.

(1952, 1954)

WESTERN SOLITARY

EDGED WINDS, the prairie's frozen stare,
Hung like a menace on the air.

A *We.stern Solitary* fled
On tiny feet, with outstretched head,
Lifting before it as it went
A deprecative, small lament.

Twin avocet wheeled rudely 'round,
Springing to plumes from starveling ground,
Raking the air with scrannel creak,
Protesting hoarsely bleak, ah, bleak.

Raw gusts, the prairie's hooded gaze,
Foretold the somber autumn days.

Was there, above the darkling hill,
The murmur of a cosmic chill,
Pale memorandum from afar,
As if, upon a setting star,
Wings and winds conspired to be
Heralds of misanthropy?

(Autumn, 1960, 1965)

AUTUMN, 1961

ONCE, WHEN I PAUSED to ponder
The thin, clear stars of night,
I turned each time the fonder
To you and evening light.

Now, when I pause, returning,
My hand upon the gate,
Inside, in each dim corner,
The chill and silence wait.

(1961)

O LABORED YEARS

O LABORED YEARS, meticulous and wan,
Paled by the long, contemptuous common glare,
Why wait in wings, denied, denying there,
The brazen gong that brings the players on?

The gilded veil reluctantly descends,
The play, the players, all disperse in doubt;
Then in the wings the watcher spies them out,
And lo! the selfsame cue for each attends.

Anticipation in the past, and past
What was consented to; now shortened breath,
Such dignity as may inhere in death,
Serenity, yea, slumber, at the last.

(1962)

A LAST LOSS

SMALL LOSSES at each step; replaceable
At first; until, in time, less loss, less gain;
Until in time there's even less to lose.
Even the last long loss comes not in vain;
For last, there's neither gain nor loss to lose.

(1965)

COUNT DOWN

ROUTINE, RENUNCIATION, resignation:
Such the summing and the sequence;
Of these the last is hardest
And the hardest
Last.

(1968)

NOT COMPARABLE TO*

("For unless there is some way of thinking without analogies
and figures of speech, we are bound, sooner or later, to reach
an impasse." George Boas, *Limits of Reason).*

TWOFOLD IS THE METAPHOR; fact; factitious.
It leans on the element; the other, apart,
Encourages error, monstrous deceit,
Breeding *as ifs.* Yet something *is.*

Hold, then, to the element. Let poets fable
Man "writ as on water," life "as a flame,"
An incandescence, pale "spiritus," air;
See these as elements, not the reverse.

After seas of grief, being torn by harsh winds,
After being consumed, comes reassurance of earth,
Rock-rugged, welcoming earth,
Whereon feet be planted, wherein be rooted.

The heart as an element is—is—was—
It shares with the tides, the unfrangible air,
The dry consuming, the earth, whose it is;
Is not compared, not comparable to.

(1963, 1964)

PART VI
POEMS SINCE FIFTY
(1944-1973)

HUDSON RIVER IDYLL*

SOUTHWARD ONE TURNED from ancient Beverwyck
And held the Hudson's west bank half a day.
Paasbloemies promised spring; the flint-hard corn
In fall made *suppawn*, and *oliekoek* spelled cruller.
Dutch words, Dutch farms, slow with the barns and chores,
The calves, the stone-walled pastures, cutting wood,
Knitting and churning, baking, winding clocks;
So ran the generations. Indian wars,
The Revolution and the Renters' quarrel,
Could not unhinge the pattern of their ways.

    Two aging sisters lingered here, alone,
Hugging their slender patrimony close,
The house and farm, rare linen, Delft-blue plate;
Paying a neighbor boy to milk their cows
And stack the wood before the winter snows.
Often their steps sought out the knoll where slept
The family past: The Hallenbecks, Van Loons
And Van den Bergs; and great-grandfather Klauw
Who'd crossed from Kinderhook in Indian times
For better land. And musing on these stones,
They drew contentment from their calm, believing
That what had lingered thus a hundred years
And more must lend some patience for their need,
Some shift to outstare dread oblivion.

    And then the century's end, and on their hearts
They knew the gropings of a chill surmise.
"How many leaves have drifted on this path,"
They said, "since father, sleeping on this knoll,
Was born in seventeen ninety-two; and we
Alone are left; and we shall rest there soon."
And through the winter months they'd knit and rock
While patiently the minutes ticked away,
And silence crowded 'round. The isinglass
Glowed cheerful on the little windowed stove.
The coals would settle with a sudden sound
Like mimic volleys on the dozing ear,
Like tiny avalanches of the hours.
And then the clock would whir the bedtime theme.

"Not yet. Not yet," they'd sigh. "Someday we'll sell.
We mustn't rush. There isn't any rush.
We'll make the buyer promise us our plot
In perpetuity. They say all that
Can be arranged. A deed will make it clear."
And nodding, comforted, they'd rise for bed,
Sleeping in winter in the nearest room;
Too cold upstairs until the lilacs leafed.

And then they sold. A new American,
Poltowski, rugged, barrel-chested, young,
A peasant bluntness in his speech, paid cash.
"But you will promise us? You will not move
The graveyard plot, will leave it on the knoll,
The stones upright, the wall around the graves?"
"Ja, sure, I don' move in until you're gone.
Dis place, I like. I build me big new barn.
I get me cows, a bull, a pick-up truck.
Ja, sure, I sign my name. I keep him good."

Thus in due time the sisters flickered out.
A few old neighbors came in carriages.
The small procession climbed the well-worn path.
The Dominie pronounced the solemn words.
The peasant moved and prospered, had his barn,
His herd, his dairy truck, his sloping lawn,
Learned English, sent his surly cubs to school.
The orchard plot was filled; the tale was told.

Strange, then, the sullen vintage of the grave,
The odd discordant fruitage of their hope:
Within the orchard lies the sunken square;
The briars fret old names no longer called;
The shadowed slabs are dim beneath the birch;
And this: wrist-thick the poison ivy grows,
Like tall young trees not easily pushed aside;
And soon the restless swine will breach the wall,
Rooting at will among the soundless past,
Mute dust, that senses no indignities.

(1948)

59

TEACHING HENRY JAMES AT N.Y.U.*

RIVERSIDE PARK: Here, text absorbed,
I sift the theme of Strether, am he
Alone on a bench in the Luxembourg.
The hot tires scuff unseen below;
The twilight deepens upon my page.

Ambassador, too, to indifferent youth,
Musing, the same in age, in mood,
I ponder Strether's ironic hour,
Gotham to West as Paris to Woolett.

An Innes sky shrouds the Jersey shore.
A cruiser glides, noiseless, up the river.
The city, unheeded, sinks to a whisper.
All is suspended in a sudden oddness
Of sameness, reluctant light the same.

(1949, revised 1966)

NOTES MÉTAPHYSIQUES*
(For Richard Wilbur)

1. *North Pole*
   Spin here and taste the fabled goal,
   here where all chase congeals;
   the trembling compass points no pole,
   and even ardor kneels.

   Small spark, alas, in shattering cold,
   the sky a tongueless black,
   and all winds south—pray sinew hold,
   brain clear, to stagger back.

2. *Bathysphere*
   Drowning to seek in opaque halls
   we stare with queasy eyes;
   though heart protest the triple walls

the fish show no surmise;
deep and darkness blend in one,
down is controverse to sun.

3.   *Altitude*
The laboring lungs rake the thin air,
the sun-tranced eyelids nod,
belly, too, craves a humbler fare,
and slow the pistons plod.

The heart shreds lean on such pinched food;
now, on the darkening rock,
shadows provoke a sober mood,
a fumbling at the lock.

Coda
Cry then each man, despise not bread
nor breathe contemning earth,
but conjugate by flesh and head
the jointures of our birth.

(1952, 1953)

PAST'S PERSISTING*

ARREST THIS Now, this fluid presentness,
this Is that's now; compel it this, not that.
Carve one cohesive, pure precipitate
pendant of instancy, jewel of here,
a crystal, blue-flame point in the ear of Now.
Borrow the painter's mode, commanding sense
to prick the nag of Time and seize the reins
of pulse and blood.
                        Establish so this tree,
this pleasant turf, this sun-bathed air, this bird
embroidering the margins of the dawn;
single and aim the eye, so stalk the Now—
but pointing thus, who flushes restless Then,
upstart, ill-timed, imposing Once on Here,
intruder Past, old memory's cicatrix?

Thus on the gray and ruminant tablet grows
a grassed expanse, a park-like citron green,
level and wide, and stabbed with slender boles
that lean in rows, and look with tender leaves
on spring, shining and soundless, innocent,
with sober sky among the stems, as if
the sun were late; nothing that should dismay;
but lone as unsigned lines on naked walls.

So the intruder Was, kenneled with Is,
persistent hound that leaps the brittle years,
splinters the fragile frame whose present edge
crumbles, dissolves. Who'll trap the fleeting Now?

(1951, 1954)

HOUSE IN SALEM

THE SHOWER HURRIES all the length of bay,
Is chased by tiny million-mirrored suns,
Takes wing, and scurries over Marblehead.
Inside, the ancient chairs stretch forth their arms
In mute dispassion, formal, chaste; for were
They not Nathaniel's throne? Portrait, his cousin,
With guileless hands and placid eyes, presides.
The stamen of draperies astounds;
And wrinkled, wavering window-panes outlast
The frosted centuries. Here Hepzibah,
Meek wraith, and Phoebe murmur; and the Judge,
Figure or fact, yet drinks the welling blood.

Shadow and sunlight are fickle things, and slight.
Timbers, preserved in sedatives of musing,
Define Nathaniel's choice of long withdrawal,
His tryst with law, necessity's cool chain.

Nathaniel might have said it: Gilt and drapes
Fade fast—gobbets of rag and shrouds of thread;
The dampish beams, like family trees, grow sick
Of dust's dull stench. Cupboards exhale of graves,
And seats of chairs are roped, and fend off faith.
Hepzibah peers no more, undone by time,
And Phoebe's silvery laugh is weird and thin
Behind the screen. Not having heeded Holgrave's
"Nothing that's mouldy will I love," old Pyncheon's
Upwelling blood rots in the caverned past.

Clouds mass for rainpelts on the bay, trees sway,
Small wavelets flash their mirrors at the sun.
Flow, light. What rests is rust; what lives is change;
Beauty of change and anodyne of flow.
No rite shall surrogate the living pulse,
The sanative of change, the restless bay.

(1952, 1955)

OLD MEN LONG DYING *

How long shall man's remembrance last on tongues,
From mouth to mouth, cheating the spade and stone?
By touch, by simple words for memory,
By long report, so might the span be stretched.
Grandson of death by arrow, born beneath
Terror of Mohawks, sixteen hundred and ninety;
Standing erect, seventeen eighty-two,
To toast the general's visit; and great-grandson
Close in the crowd; he then to his nineties, saying:
"And on this very head (touching gray temples,
Grandmother wide-eyed witness at his knee)
Washington laid his hand." And so to me.

Old men, long time a-dying, with me shall you die?
And where shall I seek my maneuver for time?
If I have dined with heroes, I had not known it.
Shall I say: "I have heard fierce winds on the spaces,
Have spied on the coyote curled and asleep in the forest,
Seen stately marching of deer (I sat on the rock)?"
Or point to shelves, announcing, "These I've read?"
Show tags of scribbled notes and minutes filed?
Shall I say: "Here (producing fragments), here
Is my card, my anonymous comment here?"

Our antique stalwarts fade. New wilderness
Extends within, and prudence pleads with judgment.
Our heroes, knowing resistance wavers, conscious
That flesh is frail, husband their courage, waiting.
Yes, there was virtue, old, old men. We praise
Endurance, regret remembrance lost, though we
Can not so simply state our foe, so clearly
Rise in courage on the uncrowded sky.
Yet tallest granites, crumb by crumb, must yield,
And you, being praised, accept inscrutable silence.

(1953, 1977)

64

EIGHTEENTH CENTURY AMERICAN
(In 18th century manner)

See throned upon the chaste Augustan chair
The *philosophe* with sage, enlightened air;
The sparse frame wrapped in cloth of sober gray
Whose flowing tails the narrow shanks display,
The scant-filled, stockinged calf, still elegant,
The buckled breech, the buckled shoe aslant;
The hair drawn tight and ribboned for the queue,
The eyes and brow refined by Reason's view;
The body trim, as fits the age of sense,
Secure in Nature's firm benevolence.
The nervous hand, the slender finger, see
Commend the opened book upon the knee;
While framed in brass, astride the scholar's nose,
Great Franklin's gift invites the mind's repose;
True Reason's token, joined with Nature's plan,
That optic laws discerned can succour man.
Thus Science follows brain, as fear the ape,
And from each minor ill provides escape.
As confidence rebukes the fool's complaint,
So books record the judgment's calm restraint;
The past the teacher, and the future taught,
Experience th'unerring nurse of ought.
Who doubts, thus armed, the sequent Golden Age
Whose hand has but to turn th'auspicious page?

(1953)

65

THREE SCORE

I HAVE NOT FAWNED on power with itching hand,
Nor humbly palmed the condescending crumb,
Nor, self-erasing, backward crawled with dumb
And servile face. Nor made I much demand,
Knew no excessive fever to expand,
But lived within the calculable sum,
And mildly marched to my own measured drum,
Patient, as thousands must be in the land.
These things are homespun, part of leveled days;
No private merit ours, within this frame,
For taming thus a mortal thirst.
Why lurks the ember ash, then, in the maze
Of flat, insipid paths, still seeking flame,
Still flushed for fire before the dull heart burst?

(1954)

LITTLE GRANDSON

TOGETHER FROM the cliff we spy
The dwindled, strange-familiar house,
Together laugh to hear the dry
Small thunder of the startled grouse,
        Little grandson.

Far off we mark the Yellowstone,
And scour the nearer knoll for flints,
Exclaim upon the great bleached bone,
And trace the tiny, two-pronged prints,
        Little grandson.

And where the soughing warm-wind pine
Leans on the valley of the brook,
We dodge the sun's relentless shine,
And try the legend of a book,
        Little grandson.

While far above, the hovering hawk
Draws lazy lines against the light,
Till four-year old, too tired to walk,
Begs piggy-back across the height,
    Little grandson.

Filtered through that untainted gaze,
A new-old glow lies over all;
And you'll store strength for dimmer days,
And I'll sleep sounder, come nightfall,
    Little grandson.

                                         (1954)

AFTERNOON TEA

THE PHRASE had been sheer chance, unnoted,
    Except that silence fell
Between these two, while voices floated
    Like echoes in a well.

A woman's eyes went cold as granite,
    Pain self-pitying, bleak;
A man's compassion strove with surfeit,
    And yet he did not speak.

As if she'd dropped a black-browed bar
    And launched a bitter spear;
As if he'd raised a rusted shield
    Against a further tear.

No doubt she'd not forgiven fate,
    Yet blamed the man somehow;
No doubt he'd searched himself for blame,
    Forbearing protest now.

Small talk went veering other rounds;
    No one had missed the two,
No one had sensed the opened wounds,
    No one had offered rue.

By such faint hints and signs as these
    As scarce to most appear,
Are bared the awful ravages
    Of love and fear.

                                         (1954)

DYLAN THOMAS

Poor Dylan drowned his pain in drink. The shock
Is such that all the literate tourists flock
To sample, in the selfsame ale and bar,
The darker sorrows of a fallen star.

(1953)

HILLS AND PLAINS

If hills contained the winds
And plains lay calm and still,
Should we prefer to climb,
Or hold the plains until
We mildewed in our minds?

(1954)

MALTHUS IN THE PARK

Italics of hunger, importunate O's,
A thousand fish-mouths yawn at the pier,
Insistent bellies, gasping their woes,
Malthus in omen uplifted here.

O prodigal human, give of your plenty,
A crumb at least, and exorcise
This slimy, existentialist scandal,
This theme for loveless lullabies.

Consider, then. old Greek good sense:
Its *meden agan,* never too much,
Rome's *ne quid nimis,* of any one thing,
Even of charity, even such.

(1965)

RIGHT TO PROTEST

Brisk on the pole, the shining flag
Provoked the temper of the crowd.
A few 'peace-lovers' raised the cry
To burn this insult on the sky;
No longer would they tolerate
The tyranny of flag and state.

Just then there burst a conic cloud
That scattered youth, and wounded eight,
Distributed the meeting-hall—
You couldn't tell the roof from wall—
And shredded colors to a rag.

'Twas then that Leeke, the young folk's choice,
Rose from the mud to lift his voice,
Demanding protest, not debate.
Indignant youth, on that brave day,
Rebuked old Nature's careless way.

(1966)

BOOK ON A WINTRY EVE

The furnace feuds with winter's chill;
The freeze is prowling at the door.
Give thanks for coal and copper still,
Mechanic allies in our war.

Books are a subtler sort of flame:
Mind kindling mind, creative spark,
Cool against cool, an inner claim,
Sagacious wrestling with the dark.

Not here the fool's illusory plea
For barren dreams, that old deceit,
But trial of mind's alacrity
At sorting clues the senses meet;

A portion of Promethian fire,
Hoarding of fuel in earnest play—
At least, until the coals expire—
To forge Frost's "momentary stay."*

(1971)

* *Frost spoke of poetry as "a momentary stay against confusion."*

69

ASPEN LEAF*

THAT WAS NO COMMON DAY. The very hills
Exulted in the autumn sun; and high
The lakes winked back the blue code of the sky.
The sky was tall; and all the streams and rills
Ran shouting down the gorges, clear and cool,
And rushed with laughter on a wide ravine
Stippled with granite, sage, and evergreen,
And darkly shining, moved from pool to pool.
The sun thrust shafts of light between the pine,
And coolly warm, the air excited like a wine.

An aspen grove ambushed the sun. At noon,
In saffron circumfusion, there it stood
Like bugles tonguing banners from the wood.
Between the boles, the aisles lay deeply strewn
With tapestries of gilt. The roof was gold,
And in the widened stream a rust-gold moss
Mimicked upon the stones a copper gloss.
Such spendthrift blaze no casual wood could hold.
It was as if upon the valley floor
A gold pavilion rose with rivers at its door.

So still, so tempered was this autumn day,
Forgot were winds and winter's mindless snow.
Softly a single yellow leaf let go
And skimmed the air, veering its vagrant way
Until it rested weightless on the grass,
And blending, vanished in the carpet's gleam.
One leaf, the fribble of an autumn theme,
Winnowed from all the millions that must pass,
By luck, emerging from the countless whole
To play its exit in a small, insensate role.

For, with the wind's premonitory rush
The autumn pigments tarnish, fade and fall,
The dead leaves chafe against the canyon wall,
The arctic stars congeal the valley's hush.
What then more brittle than the golden leaf?
A moment's hovering on the lambent air,

A spark's swift launching on the brush-fire flare,
Too paltry for the platitudes of grief.
Since leaves will waste and rot in wintry rain,
No remedy denies the cumulative stain.

We are the leaves. We shiver in our storms;
Tremulous, blotched, for all our brave parade,
Swept by the holocausts ourselves have made,
Docile in trenches, tricked by gilded forms,
The first chill blast will churn us like debris.
Rash man, in violence squandering his years,
So briefly proud, so trapped in aimless fears,
Malicious, mean, cynic in charity,
His wily brain soon panicked, body frail,
Like to the leaf, how shall his tiny gleam prevail?

Think on the dead in graves themselves have dug,
The unclean bondage, and the bully's lash,
The handy bargains in cremated ash,
And say we cancel murders with a shrug?
That boots and fists should blur the human face,
That flesh should be so less than clod, than leaf,
This is the sordid jest that no belief,
No spent, evasive promise can erase.
These monsters still are man, lust of our lust;
The stench from our own hands is Hiroshima's dust.

Heavy the tax we pay for being man:
To grope behind the shufflers on our stage,
To strain between the lines upon our page,
Wrestling within the narrows of our span
Because of this that links us with the leaf;
Subjecting dreams remorselessly to act,
Mistrusting fantasy, perplexed by fact;
If faiths betray, preferring disbelief;
Aware that hopes are froth if none seek proof;
And still the sky's infinitudes stave in our roof.

Perchance, behind the Snowy Range, one day
A silent grove sprang into subtle flame,
And having been, proved that it had a name.

Coinage of earth, reclaimed by earth's low clay,
This leaf of gold, this dart of earth and air,
Though vanity beneath the peak's cold frown,
Though drifting so, irresolutely down,
Was splendor still, until the branch was bare;
And in the sunlight, just before the blast,
Shone with a reckless grace, it may be not the last.

(1951, 1951)

CAVE WITH MARKINGS*

ALONE I STRODE the narrow gorge, alone
Came threading through the broken stone,
Paced the faint deer-trail, forced the clinging thorn,
Clambered the talus slope and clung along
The scanty shelf; until at late midmorn,
Where leaned the dead tree's sturdy prong,
I gained the shallow cave and paused for rest.
Only the rodent's droppings on the floor,
Only the runnels that the waters wore,
Only the hawk's now long abandoned nest –
Until upon the ragged limestone wall,
I spied the red man's fading red-clay scrawl.

Long ages since, between this ledge and pine,
He saw the same blue-distant snow-capped line,
The self-same wide and sunswept plain below.
Fasting, perhaps, obedient to old lore,
He mused for hours on how the eagles soar,
How rabbits change their coats for drifting snow,
How wolves outwit the fleetness of the deer;
By day, he waited out the rim-rocked sun,
By night, outstared the stars, concealing fear,
And then, exhausted, in a fevered dream
Seized on a name and traced his victory there,
His signature, the bison and the bear.

72

Far savage brother, you could scarcely know
The fateful metaphor can only grow
From the senses' slow accumulated store.
Canker one's days and mortify one's nights,
Still, from the silence of the heights,
The flesh will be your closest counselor.
The symbols of our search are launched impure,
The accents of our earthbound ears and eyes
Dictate, and memory culls what shall arise.
Analogy's a mirror's slanted lure:
As if, and as it were, for all our care,
Are body's shift, not edicts from the air.

Back in a shaded, dim primeval day,
How sense-ends quivered to the things that slay;
Then everywhere the lonely novice, man,
Eluding tusk and claw and lidless power,
Hid him as hunted; and in his hunted hour,
Small wonder if his farthest image-span
Lagged with the lion and the victim's groan.
The Asian mumbled over ivoried bone;
The Assyrian filed before the winged bull;
Even the primal cities of the Nile
Projected power in the crocodile,
And begged the serpent's stare be merciful.

When man-gods flourished on the mountain sites,
They bred and lusted by quite regal lights.
Forgot Bubastes, gone the golden calf;
Then on the hilltops, wakeful till the day,
Some midnight watcher groped his way to teach
The tribal-father tongue, the shepherd's speech;
As if one heard our western sheepman say:
"My comfort is the great sheepherder's staff;
I shall not lack; he'll find me prairie grass,
Make clean the water holes, lead on the hills,
Guard from the coyote and the wind that chills,
Shield from the loco-weed and swamp-morass,
Comfort me through the sheep-dip's rude canal
For my own good, and find me good corral."

Emblems of the hunter pale and turn profane.
Rough tradesmen, anxious for their ships and flocks,
Find Alpha in the gentled ox;
Or frame from polar-star and planets' sweep
The mighty motions of the changeless deep.
The beasts slink back; the silent spheres remain;
And sages, pondering old Euclid's lines,
Read order in the universal signs.
Thus from the gasping ages, bestial, drear,
Looms a new logos, fruitful twin event,
Lucretian Law, Judean Testament,
Each the prophetic talisman for fear.

From the outposts of the eagle and the bear
We taunt the stars to echo to our shout,
We plan a light to put the sun's light out,
And scream on wings of flame across the air.
What law is imaged in this cindered ash?
What mirrored love springs from this cobalt flash?
The vaulted silence answers like a weight;
And in a cleft once trod by savage feet,
I hear the murmur of my own blood-beat,
I trace the guesswork of my postulate.
And now as I turn to see the waning light,
Hunger and thirst rebuke the pensive flesh,
And shadows of the aspen, sharp and fresh,
Stretch their familiar fingers toward the night.

(1954)

74

PART VII
LATE HARVEST
(Since 1973)

AT LEAST

I MAY NOT RIVAL Dick and Harry
Nor rise above the ordinary,
   But still alive
   At eighty-five,
At least I've been contemporary.

(Ditto at ninety-five)

APPROACHETH NOW

Approacheth now the eightieth year.
Let us then be direct, not needing guile,
Less awed by panaceas, credos, claims,
Infuriate crowds, eddies of angry fists.

No man escapes fatality of self,
Of being, person, character, what you will,
That circumscribes his deeds, delimits choice.

Portent of modern minds, Lucretius wrote:
Man was not given hands that he might grasp,
But having hands, he grasps. We will to reach,
And thus hypothecate that will is free;
But grasping fire, earn insolence of scars,
Or touching sand, find naught to nourish us.
Wisdom is but the hard-earned core of caution,
Forged in the furnace of too ardent greeds.

A grisly figure loomed, the fable runs,
Above my lady's bed, so that she quaked,
"What will you do to me?" And it replied,
"Lady, why question me? The dream *is yours.*"
So looms the world, present, impersonal,
Ignoring us, till trial and error, thought,
And time, bring us to ask how much is ours,
How much the consequence of deeds we chose.

Old Homer, in a warrior age, declared,
"Nothing endures except the enduring heart."
So men against the ultimate wall have sworn.
Pale victims of the concentration camps
Consoled them with an ancient Stoic theme
That attitudes, at least, were ours to choose.
But now the vicious probe the very brain
To prove that worst no less than best persists.

Respect the searching mind, the sense of others,
Likeness that binds us all, yet difference
Of each, the fortitude that lasts the hour,
The briefness yet infinitude of time.

Of contradictions all that is is born.
Uncertainty will haunt our best. We end
Accepting doubt. The having lived is all.

(1972)

BOY, MAN, AND ROCK
(A Memory)
(Time, 1905, up-state New York)

BOY TRACED THE SOUND among the pines and elms:
Behind the church; man in a grave, tap-tapping
Upon a boulder four feet through. He'd dug
The grave around it, neatly framed the rock;
Then turned, head bare, his sleeves rolled high, intent,
His gray panache pert as a blue-jay's crest,
To pit his puny will upon the great
Ice-age itself, immortalized in stone.
At each dull tap his hammer-sledge bounced back,
Old man indulging in a whim, that seemed
More futile as it promised no result
Beyond the eccentricity itself.

Two hours had passed when boy returned and paused.
No change, he saw, except a thin, gray dust
Along the boulder where the sledge had bounced.

77

But man still pecked away, not sweating, calm,
A tireless elf defying earth's own seal.
He cocked an eye at boy and read his thought,
And spoke in rhythm with his steady taps,
"They'll crack," he said. "Just give 'em plenty time."

Boy watched. Man tapped away, relentless, firm.
The gaunt, round-shouldered tombstones leaned to look.
The grass beside the paths, the glistening pines,
The half-way sun, the very trees and sky
Hovered in limpid light and peace. And then
The boulder fell apart, like opened palms
Of granite gray, dull planes as surly still
As was the parent fist, but in consent.

A slow, confirming nod was all that seamed,
Sagacious face could grant his foe. Man leaned
A moment on his sledge to contemplate
The halves, still more than his lone strength could heave.
Down in the hole, the grave, one with the earth,
He spoke. "The rest comes easier," he said.
Then grim, as if a boy should see the sense,
Pronounced, "I was with Grant at Petersburg."

(1970)

FIVE HAIKU*

RAINY AFTERNOON INDOORS

PLASH of sudden drops;
Murmurs from the dripping leaves:
Scholar, turn the page.

JAPANESE GARDEN

BRIDGE and shadowed path,
Shouldered rock and sun-flecked pool;
Lose the restless self.

MISTY MOON OVER IOWA

GHOSTS of red men rise;
Roam beneath dew-misted trees:
Sigh, for past that dies.

SPRING JEWEL

WHITE in snow, the tree
Flaunts its one bright garnet gem:
Bold, the robin's breast.

(c. 1975)

NOVEMBER
SAY IT with a sigh:
The last leaf has drifted by;
Wintry is our sky.

(1981)

NEWTON'S APPLE*

ON NEWTON'S PATE, quite by surprise,
An apple fell – you know the rest:
A brain, accustomed to surmise,
There launched upon a cosmic quest.

I heard by chance a Ph.D.
Demean this legend as a joke,
A mildew of mythology.
The kind that flatters foolish folk.

But genius moves in ways unique,
Is swift to pounce upon a clue;
A *multa paucis*, so to speak,
From little, great things may ensue.

What else can apples do but fall
To earth, if naught else intervene?
This query stimulates recall,
The role of gravity foreseen.

II
(The argument)
A gust of wind diverts by brief assault,
A good right arm projects as instrument,
A bullet's parabolic flight – but halt!
Here mathematics lends its argument.

The more projective force, the further course,
Each parallel to earth till power is spent;
Earth's pull, that is, when countermet by force,
Suggests the glue that binds the firmament.

The planet earth, then viewed as sun-revolved,
Has brewed a philosophic thunderbolt;
Denying chance, old miracles dissolved,
Our apple's dealt mankind a cosmic jolt.

Now Newton broods upon the interim:
How Reason challenges the time-worn tales;
How mathematic Law replaces whim,
And order universally prevails.

CODA

Apologize, young sir; you've lost your case.
You denigrated legend all too soon;
Thank Newton: ships now cruise in outer space,
And Yankee boots now tread Diana's moon.

(1985; rev. 1989)

HECUBA TO HANNAH DUSTIN*

PURITAN HOUSEWIFE on a grim frontier,
Doubtless she'd never heard of Hecuba;
Or even if she had, what's Hecuba
To her, or she to Hecuba, that she
In Haverhill should that fallen queen bewail?
Enslaved to Greeks, ragged, derided, shorn
Of children, husband slain; fairest of daughters
An offering on Achilles' tomb; last son,
Left safe with Thrace's king, brought to her arms
A small, surf-pounded corpse – and she, cold hate,
Gouged out the false king's eyes and slew his sons;
And for her deed turned to a slavering bitch.

And what of Hannah, Hannah Dustin, bedded
With week-old child, by howling Indians snatched,
Half-clad, in snow and mud and one foot bare,
Herded a hundred twenty pitiless miles?
The laggards tomahawked with one swift swing,
Her baby's brain splattered against a tree,
Her husband, children, left and mourned for dead.
And when encamped, the boasts of coming sport:
Each to be scourged, stripped bare, the gauntlet run,
Fiends' tortures, knives, and glee at victim's cries.

The warriors guard the tent, with squaws and
young.
In darkest night she seizes tomahawks,
With one lad's help, and smashes savage skulls;
Half fainting, staggering south in pathless woods,
Gropes back to Haverhill, ten scalps as proof,
To find her husband, children, safe and well.

Hecuba's tale is legend, Hannah's fact.
Did neighbors whisper, pointing, as she passed?
"What would you do?" she might with Hamlet plead,
"Had you the motive and the cue for passion?"
Pitted against such odds, infirm, alone,
No power, no precedent, no priest, no law?
Amaze the pulpit, and confound the Saints?
Had they been men, their names had been renowned.

Euripides left Justice to the Fates.
Timothy Dwight, true Calvinist, had doubts:
"Intrepid, yes, but what of rectitude?"
He chose, instead, to weigh the husband's plight:
Whether 'twere nobler in the man to suffer
The slings and arrows of outrageous fortune,
Or by opposing save the children, leave
Mother and babe, cabined and cribbed, to God
And "noble" savages. His choice was hard.
But Hannah, Hecuba, pushed to the rim,
Took Justice to themselves. Heroic deeds –
But bitch or brave, they tasked the hallowed creeds.

(1979, 1980)

THREE SONNETS FROM HEREDIA.*

(See Addenda for French Sonnets)

THE TOILER

THE SEEDER, PLOW, a yoke, the plowshare's shine,
The harrow, goad, the sickle, honed and keen,
That in one day the plot's corn-ears will glean,
The fork that spreads the grain with wooden tine;

These long familiar tools, this day too heavy grown,
Old Parmis vows them to immortal Earth
Beneath whose sacred soil the seed finds birth.
His task is done; his four-score years have flown.

A century in the sun, no wealth for yield,
He pushes his plow across the fallow field;
No joy in life, grows old without regret.

Weary of working clods, foregoing thanks,
He dreams that even dead, he's plowing yet
The shadowed glebe on Erebean banks.

THE STAINED-GLASS WINDOW

THIS STAINED-GLASS LIGHT has viewed high dames and lords,
Gleaming with gold and azure, pearl and flame,
Heeding the hand of kings who gave them name,
Bow low their pride of crests, their hoods and swords.

They rode to sound of horns, or bugles on the night,
Brave blade in hand, gerfalcon or the hawk,
Toward plain or woods, Byzance, or Saint-Jean d'Acre,
To far Crusades, or herons in their flight.

Today the manor lords beside their ladies fine
On marble slabs of black and white recline,
A greyhound at their feet of pointed toes;

So signless, voiceless, deaf, still lying there,
With eyes of stone that no more see, they stare
Beyond the window's ever-flowering rose.

THE FORGOTTEN

THE TEMPLE LIES in ruins atop the promontory.
And death has intermingled, in his grey terrain,
The marble goddesses, the brazen heroes slain,
Entombed, beneath the solitary turf, their glory.

Alone, the herdsman drives his oxen to the spring,
Upon his conch-shell breathing some antique refrain,
Filling the quiet heavens, across the spreading main;
And on the endless blue his form lifts darkening.

Sweet Mother Earth, remembering ancient gods, forthwith,
Each spring, though eloquent in vain, still interweaves
Upon the shattered column new acanthus leaves;

But man, indifferent to old ancestral myth,
Can hear without a qualm, in nights serene, profound,
Old Ocean mourning still the Siren's honeyed sound.

(Autumn, 1975)

SOUL*
(An Exercise in Semantics)

A SOUL? Morpheme, but how defined?
As *spirit, psyche*? Both a breath,
Eluding on the edge of death;
Or quaintly wee homunculus,
Entrapped somehow in each of us?
Projections, these, of mythic mind.

Unpeopling earth, soul claims quintessence:
Subsuming what it is to be
(To breathe, to feel, to muse, to see);
Impeaching flesh by metaphor,
Comes pleading at abstraction's door,
A word, a wraith, in search of essence.

Nirvana (*nis* and *vah*) means less:
Blown out, like wicks when high winds call,
To dissipate the I in all –
In I-less dark, deprived of seeing,
No trace of passion-pain of being,
Denied the ounce of consciousness.

But since we live, the proudful We
Seeks axis of identity
In archive brain, in breath, in "soul" –
Some witching word to stay the whole;
Alas, but groping *in extremis*,
Pale analogs invoked as premise.

(1978)

LUCRETIUS, GO WEST*

WANDERING ONE DAY the wide hills of Wyoming,
The grasslands, warm between shoulders of mountains
That like old sachems huddle in council,
I paused to savor this largess of distance.
Not far, on a western slope, a gray
Outcrop of rock, sandstone and lime,
Spread thinly, oval in shape, much like
A giant amoeboid, pseudopodia stretching.

But look! A false foot extends itself slowly;
The main mass creeps, as if to absorb it.
I seize my glasses – lo! sheep that go grazing!
No rock-bound unit, but senses deceptive.
This image that teases my mind, insistent,
What metaphors linked, what cosmic allusion?

Arma virumque cano – but why hexameters pulsing,
Echoes of once mighty Rome, remote from heights and the
    herdsman?
I seek a man and a premise; and Virgil fails to give answer.

Home to my backlog of books – ah, here, *De Rerum Natura*;
Atoms that flow, creating, old fears and night overcoming.
Like not my thesis, says he? Propose then one that is better.

Omnia cum rerum primordia sint in motu:
Since all primal elements of things, that is, atoms,
Are in motion, then, surely, *non est mirabile*,
'Tis not to be wondered at if the grand total
As one in stillness seems standing.
For the nature of primal things, *Primorum Natura*,
Lies hidden beneath our senses, *ab sensibus infra.*

Thus oft on a hillside, *saepe in colli*,
The wool-bearing sheep go creeping, *lanigerae reptant*,
As the grassy slopes will tempt them, *invitant herbae*,
But to us at a distance are seen as a blur,
Nobis longe confusa videntur,
And as whiteness, that halts on green hills,
Et velut in viridi candor consistere colli.

Ah, Lucretius, hill-wanderer thou,
Student of heavens and earth and causes,
Time has revenged you, outcast as you were;
For Boyle and Newton, Locke and Gassendi,
Filched from your store, flung open the modern.
All inwardly seethes, atoms in motion, falling,
Combining, decombining; planets not spirits
But material; myths of the past made folly.

O genus infelix humanum, unhappy the human tribe,
Who follow false idols still. *Sed mage*, but rather,
Piety is *pacata posse omnia mente tueri*,
To be able to view the ALL with a quiet mind.

(1974, 1974)

EXIT?

ENERGY, said my freshman physics text,
Though not created, not destroyed, selects
To recombine in multivaried ways,
Beyond computing in our short-lived days.

Per-chance I'll share my pittance with a rose,
Per-chance a weed, a root, the grass that grows.
Be thankful, friends, for that great donor, sun,
Without which Life on earth had ne'er begun.

(1990)

ADDENDA
LE TOMBEAU D'EDGAR POE
By Stephane Mallarmé*

TEL QU'EN LUI-MÊME ENFIN l'éternité le change,
Le Poète suscite avec un glaive nu
Son siècle épouvanté de n'avoir pas connu
Que la mort triomphait dans cette voix étrange!

Eux, comme un vil sursaut d'hydre oyant jadis l'ange
Donner un sens plus pur aux mots de la tribu
Proclamèrent très haut le sortilège bu
Dans le flot sans honneur de quelque noir mélange

Du sol et de la nue hostiles, ô grief!
Si notre idée avec ne sculpte un bas-relief
Dont la tombe de Poe éblouissante s'orne

Calme bloc ici-bas chu d'un désastre obscur
Que ce granit du moins montre à jamais sa borne
Aux noirs vols du Blasphème épars dans le futur.

*Mallarmé, *Poésies*, 22nd edition, Paris, 1921, 132.

Three sonnets from Heredia's *Les Trophées*

LE LABOUREUR*

Le SEMOIR, LA CHARRUE, un joug, des socs luisants,
La herse, l'aiguillon et la faulx acérée,
Qui fauchait en un jour les épis d'une airée,
Et la fourche qui tend la gerbe aux paysans;

Ces outils familiers, aujourd'hui trop pesants,
Le vieux Parmis les voue à l'immortelle Rhée
Par qui le germe éclôt sous la terre sacrée.
Pour lui, sa tâche est faite; il a quatre-vingt ans.

Près d'un siècle, au soleil, sans en être plus riche,
Il a poussé le coutre au travers de la friche;
Ayant vécu sans joie, il vieillit sans remords.

Mais il est las d'avoir tant peiné sur la glèbe
Et songe que peut-être il faudra, chez les morts,
Labourer des champs d'ombre arrosés par l'Erèbe.

VITRAIL

Cette VERRIÈRE A VU dames et hauts barons
Étincelants d'azur, d'or, de flamme et de nacre,
Incliner, sous la dextre auguste qui consacre,
L'orgueil de leurs cimiers et de leurs chaperons,

Lorsqu'ils allaient, au bruit du cor ou des clairons,
Ayant le glaive au poing, le gerfaut ou le sacre,
Vers la plaine ou le bois, Byzance ou Saint-Jean
        d'Acre,
Partir pour la croisade ou le vol des hérons.

Aujourd'hui, les seigneurs auprès des châtelaines,
Avec le lévrier à leurs longues poulaines,
S'allongent aux carreaux de marbre blanc et noir;

Ils gisent là sans voix, sans geste et sans ouïe,
Et de leurs yeux de pierre ils regardent sans voir
La rose du vitrail toujours épanouie.

89

L'OUBLI

Le temple est en ruine au haut du promontoire.
Et la Mort a mêlé, dans ce fauve terrain,
Les Déesses de marbre et les Héros d'airain
Dont l'herbe solitaire ensevelit la gloire.

Seul, parfois, un bouvier menant ses buffles boire,
De sa conque où soupire un antique refrain
Emplissant le ciel calme et l'horizon marin,
Sur l'azur infini dresse sa forme noire.

La Terre maternelle et douce aux anciens Dieux
Fait à chaque printemps, vainement éloquente,
Au chapiteau brisé verdir un autre acanthe;

Mais l'Homme indifférent au rêve des aïeux
Écoute sans frémir, du fond des nuits sereines,
La Mer qui se lamente en pleurant les Sirènes.

APPENDIX

Parts I-VI (1925-1973)

p. 4. Carl Sandburg gave one of his earlier recitals at the University of Wyoming, Feb. 1929.

p. 9. The English department fell into an informal dispute on the use of grammar, which entered into spontaneous versifying. This item concluded the incident.

p. 11. Literate readers will identify Emerson, Thoreau, Emily Dickinson, Poe, Melville, Crane's "The Open Boat," E.A. Robinson's "Man Against the Sky," Dreiser, MacLeish's "You, Andrew Marvel," Robinson Jeffers' "Night," Frost, and Whitman.

p. 14. "And Battles Long Ago" appeared in *The Literary Digest* Jan. 5, 1929.

p. 21. "Child, Man, and Watcher." "Discrete parenthesis" represents lovers withdrawn.

p. 24. "Abandoned Mining Camp" from the author's teaching in Leadville, Colo., 1922-23.

p. 26. Only later did I note that "Sheepherder's Wind" was composed in four sentences only.

p. 28. "On a Naked Hill in Wyoming" derived from a hike to the totally abandoned coal-mining camp, Cambria, near Newcastle, Wyo. It is a literal description, the bird vaguely suggesting a faint life-renewal. Published in *The Southwest Review*, it was requested in two high school texts, Lippincott and Harcourt, Brace.

p. 36. "Continental Divide" factually reported, appeared in *The American Scholar*, XV, 1946.

p. 38. "Laramie Hills" appeared in *The Saturday Review*, and has been cited elsewhere.

p. 40.   "We Borne Along," with its alternating stanzas of seven and two eight stress lines, and three eight stress lines, plus refrain in four, five in last third and final stanza, is now too obviously Sydney Lanierish as to rhythm.

p. 42.   "Antelope Creek" was in *The Pacific Spectator*.

p. 45.   The original "Blacksmiths" may be found in Kenneth Sisam's *Fourteenth Century Verse and Prose* (Oxford, 1928).

p. 46.   Roger Fry translated Mallarmé's "Le Tombeau d'Edgar Poe" in prose form. Challenged, I essayed the original sonnet form, which Edmund Wilson praised. Mallarmé's *Poésies* Paris (1921, 132).

p. 48-   Paul Valéry's "Tais Toi" appeared in *Mélange* (Paris,
49.   Gallimard, 1941, 28). This translation appeared in *Prism International*, Univ. of Brit. Columbia, 1967. "Ton Corps" was in *La Revue de la Poésie Française*, XV, 1956.

p. 52ff. Poems here reflect the death of parents, and in 1961, my wife. The last poem in this group appeared in *The Massachusetts Review* (Summer, 1964). In it, the metaphor consists of a real base, used to create an abstraction. The ancient four elements illustrate, to which is added a personal "element."

p. 58.   "Hudson River Idyll" is family history except for the Polish buyer. Beverwyck became Albany.

p. 60.   In the summer session of 1949 I taught at New York University, Washington Square, with a hovering sense of childhood memories.

p. 60.   "Notes Métaphysiques." Richard Wilbur generously read this poem during his second evening, as linked with his previous remarks as to the poet's need to return to the concrete. "Conjugation" is both joining and analysis, "jointures" joint tenancy and union. The poem was in *The Colorado Quarterly.*

p. 62. "Past's Persisting." A present concentration is always colored by deep seated memories.

p. 64. "Old Men Long Dying." Reflects family history.

p. 70. "Aspen Leaf." First Phi Beta Kappa poem to be read at the University of Wyoming spring banquet. It appeared in *The American Scholar*, 1951. Stanzas are two quatrains and a couplet, last line hexameter.

p. 72. "Cave With Markings." From a solitary hike some twenty miles northeast of Laramie, Wyo. A rude tracing on the inner wall of a cave of some larger animal, perhaps bear, launched a reflection on how metaphors arose from a concrete experience.

PART VII (Since 1973)

p. 79. "Haiku." A Japanese-English magazine defined the Haiku, sent a letter from a former student asking if I might submit some in English. I had not tried any but sent the following.

p. 80. "Newton's Apple." (The "argument" demanded a longer line.)

p. 81. "Hecuba to Hannah Dustin." Chancing to read in the same week the *Hecuba* of Euripides (Englished) and Timothy Dwight's *Travels in New England*, in which he recalled the Hannah Dustin of a century before, I brought the two together in the pentameters of Hamlet's Hecuba. Dwight cautiously called Hannah "intrepid," but what of "rectitude"? Hence he praised the husband.

p. 83. "Three Sonnets from Heredia." Jose Maria Heredia (1842-1905) was known for a single book, *Les Trophées*, consisting of 118 sonnets, strictly formed, noted for their clarity and crisp final lines.

"The Laborer" presented problems. Who was
Parmis? *The Greek-English Dictionary* said only
"Parmis, -ides, O.Ant.Pal.," which is only genitive,
masculine, "See *Anthologica Palatina*", not in our
library. The *Loeb Classics* in four volumes listed no
Parmis; the French *Rhée*, for which I wrote Earth, said
only "See Demeter, Cybele." Patient search found
in Vol. IV, 95, the original under "Dedicatory Verse"
by one Antiphilus.

The English translation supplied Heredia's Parmis,
the husbandman, resting from his sore toil dedicated
to Demeter. The original Greek read Kybele. His
tools were listed, "ox-turning goad," the bag for seed-
corn (wheat), the curved sickle, the winnowing fork,
etc. Demeter, Kybele, Heredia's Rhée (for the
rhyme) – all three are more or less goddesses of earth.
Heredia invented the "Old" and "eighty years," and
most of the sestet, though *glèbe* rhymed with the
French *Erèbe*, the fabled under-world river.

One hardly need say that a mere translation of Here-
dia is a challenge, especially in his sonnet form.

p. 84.　"Soul." This poem invades the realm of Semantics.
A morpheme, a single sound, has no meaning unless
two or more agree that it stands for some object or act
or idea (noun, verb, or metaphor). The written word
is tertiary, a symbol for a symbol. There seems no
other way to name the unseen or unknown except to
say that "it may be like" some concrete thing we
know as existing.

Latin and Greek *spiritus* and *psyche* originally meant
breath or to breathe, once thought to be the "prin-
ciple of life." "Soul" is of unidentifiable Germanic
origin. Hobbes in the 1600s wrote: "Soule and life
do usually signify the same thing." Note how the
abstract becomes, an IT, a thing.

94

Such is not theory, but fact. Words like spirit, mind, belief, can never be depicted as objects or photographed. Yet they come to be treated as entities existing in some ethereal realm.

p. 85.   "Lucretius, Go West." The two first stanzas are factual, an experience. The third is the recollection of a passage in Lucretius of the same factual observation (*De Rerum Natura*, II, 308-322). The final citation is from V, 1194-1203. The poem was published in *The Prairie Schooner* (Univ. of Neb. Spring, 1974), and in the French *Europe*, 1983.

BIOGRAPHICAL NOTE

WILSON OBER CLOUGH, long professor of English and American Studies at the University of Wyoming, was born Jan. 7, 1894. His early years were lived chiefly in the family background of Schenectady county and city. The name was originally Holland Dutch, Clauw, in the upper Hudson region since 1654.

A Phi Beta Kappa graduate of Union College in 1917, he was soon in the Field Artillery in France, in three engagements. After the Armistice, he was granted a four months' leave to study at the University of Montpellier. Returning to the States he drifted west, teaching high school Latin and English, until, M.A. from Colorado, he became an instructor in English at the University of Wyoming. Here he has led an active life, with leaves for study at Chicago and Fellow in English at Wisconsin, and summer teaching at New Mexico, Lehigh, and N.Y.U., Washington Square.

Author of numerous articles, plus reviews, poems, short stories and books, his best known books, aside from a grammar (Lippincott), and two histories of the University of Wyoming, have been his *Intellectual Origins of American National Thought*, and *The Necessary Earth*. The first of these reviewed, with citation, the libraries of the Founding Fathers. This text has twice been issued in paperback (Citadel). The second book traced the impact of the American frontier on the language and imagery in major American authors. Four books of translation from the French have also been issued, two published abroad (Faber & Faber, London, and Mouton, The Hague). *The Necessary Earth* has appeared in Japanese, Tokyo.

Poems, he says, have been less planning than impulse. The teacher of literature, like the musician, should practice on his instrument.

COLOPHON

Designed by the University of Wyoming Graphic Arts, this book is set in Caslon type. This face is traced back to the 18th century English designer, William Caslon, and was once the number one typeface among typographers. The book is printed on Glatfelter Natural 408 ppi Text, 60 lb., with matching endsheets. The cover is Holliston's Roxite blue linen finish.